Amish Cooks Across America

Amish Cooks Across America

Recipes and Traditions from Maine to Montana

KEVIN WILLIAMS AND LOVINA EICHER

PHOTOGRAPHY BY RACHEL DIVER WILLIAMS

**Andrews McMeel
Publishing, LLC**

Kansas City · Sydney · London

Andrews McMeel Publishing, LLC
an Andrews McMeel Universal company
1130 Walnut Street, Kansas City, Missouri 64106

www.andrewsmcmeel.com

13 14 15 16 17 TEN 10 9 8 7 6 5 4 3 2 1

ISBN: 978-1-4494-2109-0

Library of Congress Control Number: 2012931246

ATTENTION: SCHOOLS AND BUSINESSES
Andrews McMeel books are available at quantity discounts with bulk purchase for educational, business, or sales promotional use. For information, please e-mail the Andrews McMeel Publishing Special Sales Department: specialsales@amuniversal.com

# CONTENTS

FOREWORD

BY LOVINA EICHER, THE AMISH COOK

It is hard to believe that Kevin and I have worked on hundreds of columns and three cookbooks together. It doesn't seem like it was so long ago that I took over my mother's column and we started on our own journey, with me writing and him editing. What surprises me even more is that a lot of people still don't know about the Amish. Throughout the course of work on *Amish Cooks Across America*, I even found myself learning new things.

I love learning about the differences between one Amish community and another. When we have visitors from another Amish settlement we can sometimes pick out the different dress codes, which vary from community to community. When we lived in Indiana, we used an uncovered buggy all year. Here in Michigan, most Amish use covered buggies.

In the communities I have visited I can also see a difference in how church services are held. Whereas one community will hold church services in the main part of the house, others will hold services in the basement or a heated outdoor building. For the communities that hold church services in the main part of the house, all the furniture has to be moved. There is also a difference in the church lunches. Some communities might serve ham, beef, and cheese; others serve egg salad, cheese spread, and so forth. Foods vary a lot from community to community because we grow most of our own food and use what we have available. What is plentiful in one place may not be found at all in another.

Because it is hard to travel very far by horse and buggy, and because there is a lot to do at home, I have not traveled to many different Amish communities in other states. That has made it difficult for me to pick up on all the differences from one place to another. So Kevin had to do most of the traveling and I enjoyed reading about his journeys when he returned. Writing this book with Kevin has given me a wonderful view of the many differences between Amish and Mennonite areas all over America. It has let me see the different customs in a way I never have before.

Some of the recipes are new to me. I find it interesting to read about the different meats that are used in some Amish communities. We don't have alligators to make the Fried Alligator Nuggets (page 136), but the Barbecued Venison Meatballs (page 58) have already become a family favorite here. Recipes like the Grilled Moose Steaks (page 155), the Oatmeal Bologna (page 68), and the Shrimp Salad Sandwiches (page 36) also sound good. Before I saw the recipe for Muscadine Pie (page 116), I had never heard of muscadines. They do not grow in Michigan or in Indiana where I grew up. We make a lot of custard pies because milk is rarely in short supply here.

I hope all of you enjoy sampling the recipes in this book as much as I have, or just reading about all the different Amish customs and foods.

# INTRODUCTION

BY KEVIN WILLIAMS

Welcome to what we hope you'll find to be a fascinating culinary and cultural journey!

From my perch as editor and creator of the popular syndicated newspaper column "The Amish Cook," first written by Lovina's mother, Elizabeth Coblentz, then taken over by Lovina, I have been tasting, testing, and talking about Amish recipes for most of my adult life. For more than twenty years I've explored the culinary corridors of Amish and Mennonite culture. In the beginning I didn't know much; I just had a general sense that, first, Amish cooking was popular; and, second, assumed that an Amish menu in Jamesport, Missouri, was probably the same as one in Ephrata, Pennsylvania. On the first hunch, I was right. But the second assumption would prove to be wrong, and that is what this book explores.

My first glimpse of Amish cooking's legendary following occurred before I really even knew who the Amish were. On family trips to visit friends in Columbus, Ohio, we would always pass a couple of "Amish-style" restaurants on US Route 42 outside Plain City. Plain City, by the way, is not named so because of its geography but for its inhabitants, commonly known as the "plain people." Well, more accurately, *former* inhabitants. As nearby Columbus began to expand westward into the prime Plain City–area farmland, the Amish, who prefer more rural areas, began packing up and heading to Wisconsin and Missouri. Some say that if one looks closely enough at some aging rural roads, the ruts from old buggy wheels can still be seen in the pavement, a reminder of the area's once-thriving Amish community.

There's another reminder of the area's Amish past: restaurants. Although the Amish are long gone from the Plain City area, a handful of eateries remain, still serving dumplings, buttered noodles, panfried chicken, and other "Amish-style" cuisine. Lines of customers still queue up outside the remaining restaurants—they are probably the sons and daughters of the patrons I remember seeing as a child—waiting for the heaping helpings of buttered noodles, homemade rolls, stuffed pork chops, and for dessert, slices of pie as big as a football.

It wasn't until I was an eighteen-year-old journalism intern at my local newspaper that I actually had a meal at one of these "Amish-style" restaurants. The restaurant, outside Waynesville, Ohio, was Der Dutchman, which burned down in 2010, permanently shuttering it. Never mind that there wasn't—and still isn't—an Amish settlement within 100 miles of Waynesville; the restaurant still attracted hordes of people looking for hearty, heavy fare and Amish ambiance. As a journalist, I was in search of information about a different group of "plain people," a sect that actually does inhabit southwest Ohio: the Old German Baptist Brethren. The teenage waitress wearing a kitschy Amish-type costume knew nothing about the German Baptists, and I came away with an empty notebook but a full stomach. The Yankee pot roast and fat buttered rolls, long a staple of Amish homes, filled me up quite nicely.

With that culinary experience I joined the ranks of Americans who thought all Amish cooking was essentially the same: meat and potatoes for the main course, and butter-slathered, lard-infused, cinnamon-roll sweetness in dessert.

BEYOND SHOOFLY PIE

I learned the hard way that Amish cooking and baking weren't the same everywhere.

"Do you have any shoofly pie?" I asked an Amish woman in Indiana who was offering pie for dessert.

Instead I got a puzzled expression.

"You're kidding me? You haven't heard of shoofly pie? Isn't that like an Italian saying he's never eaten spaghetti? I thought the Amish and shoofly were synonymous."

Okay, I didn't actually say any of those things to my host. But I was thinking them.

"Heard of it, I think. But never made it or tried it," the Amish woman said.

Such dishes as shoofly pie, chicken-corn soup, and apple pandowdy are supposedly Amish cuisine. But an Amish person in Lancaster County, Pennsylvania, may have a very different menu than an Amish cook in Kansas. One misguided newspaper editor even went so far as to suggest that maybe "The Amish Cook" columnist was a fictional character because she had never made Amish Friendship Bread.

"'The Amish Cook' has never made Amish Friendship Bread?" the editor asked incredulously.

"No, she hasn't," I affirmed.

"Well, I just find this very hard to believe," the editor said.

What the editor didn't understand—and what most outsiders don't—is that Amish cooking is very different in different areas. One Amish cook's shoofly pie is another's Muscadine Pie (page 116). Sure, some foods seem to enjoy universal appreciation among the Amish (whoopie pies or pickled beets, anyone?), but other dishes that are ubiquitous in some places are unheard of by Amish in others. They are the original locavores. They grow as much of their own food as they can, and they make great use of the ingredients available to them. This book is full of such examples of local ingredients being incorporated into the Amish diet, whether it's the Elderberry Custard Pie (page 13) in Upstate New York or the moose steaks (page 155) in Rexford, Montana.

Sometimes it's more a matter of tradition than the availability of ingredients. Some traditional foods take root in one settlement but don't catch on elsewhere. Or the foods are popular, but for different reasons. For instance, in some Indiana settlements, homemade raisin pie is a popular wedding offering. Yet among the Amish in Pennsylvania, raisin pie is served so often at funerals that it has earned the moniker "funeral pie." And in some parts of Indiana, where Amish from Pennsylvania have recently moved, funeral pie can be served just 30 or 40 miles away from where another settlement has it on its wedding menu. Are you confused yet?

The fact is, most Amish people generally don't stray far from the settlement they were born in, so they're generally raised on the same foods and recipes for generations. Typically the Amish are not prolific travelers, though there are some notable exceptions (see page 104). But this same isolation creates a fascinating variety of foods. As editor of "The Amish Cook," my job has taken me to plain settlements from coast to coast, giving me an unparalleled perspective on Amish foods, and with Lovina's help and insight, I'm excited to share them here.

SIMPLE BEGINNINGS

The Amish have long captivated the world with their insistence on clinging to the ways of a seemingly bygone era. In most Amish settlements, horse-drawn carriages are still more common than cars, and electricity is something seen as a luxury enjoyed by others. Amish life is simpler in many ways: no need for car insurance, no Internet service providers to haggle with, no pressure to stay in step with the latest fashions, no struggles to pay the utility bill. But there is a trade-off; a simpler life doesn't mean an easier life. Days are long. On most Amish farms, chores begin before sunrise and continue until bedtime. Meals, however, are wholesome and hearty, and family is first among the Old Order Amish.

The Old Order Amish, along with the Mennonites and Hutterites, are members of a seventeenth-century religious movement known as Anabaptism (meaning "adult baptism"). The Amish, founded by Jakob Ammann, believed that only adults could choose their religion. They split from other mainline churches of the era that practiced infant baptism. The Mennonites, led by Menno Simons, actually initiated the split, but Ammann wanted to go further and led his flock into a very conservative, Bible-based, family-centered, pacifist order. The Hutterites, founded by Jakob Hutter around the same time, blend most of the same religious principles of the Amish and Mennonites, but they live communally.

While the Amish are often misunderstood by outsiders, they have a common "language" that all can appreciate: food. Amish meals are much different than what most outsiders think of when they hear the term "Amish cooking." Pop culture images of the Amish serving lard-laden piecrusts and thick chicken-corn soup are rooted less in reality than in tourism brochures. Amish cooking has won legions of fans for its simplicity and adherence to back-to-basics ingredients. Perhaps the Amish are most legendary for their desserts, such as their scratch-made piecrusts filled with butterscotch or creamy custard or bursting with berries while in season. Cookies, cakes, and puddings are also in the realm of any Amish cook with a sweet tooth. In reality, Amish diets are as varied and different as the settlements themselves, whether that be huckleberry milkshakes in Montana or barbecued venison meatballs in Illinois.

But there's much more. As the Amish population has increased in the United States and Canada (some estimates say their population doubles each generation—not a reach, considering their average family size of eight children), they have had to stake out new ground for their generally rural communities. There are now Old Order Amish settlements in such states as Colorado, Mississippi, New Mexico, and Maine, all venues that never knew an Amish population as recently as the year 2002.

Amish culinary culture often emphasizes local ingredients and seasonal rhythms. The Amish were locavores well before it became a trendy food phrase. So as the Amish move to places previously unknown to them, they have embraced regional and provincial foods and made them their own. In places like Tennessee and Georgia, such Southern favorites as cornbread and kale have made it onto the menu. In Montana, the Amish enjoy wild game; and in Maine, it's blueberries everywhere.

One undeniable food trend that has accelerated among the Amish (first written about in our book *The Amish Cook at Home*) is an embrace of south-of-the-border cuisine. In south Texas, the Amish began incorporating such favorites as jalapeños and cactus in their foods, and that style of cooking traveled like no other. Whether it be Quesadillas (page 71) or burritos (see page 166), a Hispanic flavor has washed over Amish cooking in almost every settlement I've visited. In many ways, though, this trend is a natural. All the ingredients to make a fresh salsa or taco-type supper can be gathered in the garden. The Hispanic influence has added a splash of spice to a historically plain-cooking culture.

Another common food trend found among the Amish is simply the influence of more store-bought foods. The Amish are no longer the insular, agrarian culture they once were. In addition to farming, many Amish work in factories, as carpenters, and cabinet makers, as greenhouse operators, and in an increasingly diverse range of other once-unthinkable occupations (see page 92).

When planning this book, it was difficult to decide whom to include. After all, Old Order Mennonite cooking and baking is quite similar to Old Order Amish. And the Beachy Amish Mennonites come from a similar culinary background. In the end, we decided to focus on "horse-and-buggy Amish."

It occurred to me that while I work with *The Amish Cook*, there are scores of other wonderful Amish cooks across America. There is Miriam Miller's melt-in-your-mouth Rhubarb Bread (page 27) in Fredonia, Pennsylvania; and Gloria Yoder's Barbecued Venison Meatballs (page 58) in Flat Rock, Illinois, offering a hint of sweet and a subtle sour while taming the meat's sometimes gamey taste. There is the homemade blueberry cake (page 16) at Elizabeth Stoll's house in Unity, Maine; and the amazing, pungent blue cheese aged to perfection in Cambria, Wisconsin (see page 83). And I'll never forget Sarah Martin's homemade Butter Tarts (page 25) in Aylmer, Ontario. I made many new friends during the journey and gained a deeper understanding of the variety of Amish culinary culture.

Some may wonder why we didn't spend much time exploring the most populous Amish settlements. That's a fair question. The largest Old Order Amish communities in the United States by population are Holmes and Wayne Counties in Ohio; Lancaster County, Pennsylvania; and the Nappanee-Shipshewana settlements of northern Indiana, according to the Young Center for Anabaptist Studies at Elizabethtown College in Pennsylvania. These settlements have been written about in innumerable textbooks, cookbooks, and blogs. In fact, they are chronicled so extensively that people often overlook the myriad of Amish settlements found elsewhere. These "other" Amish communities are diverse in their culinary traditions and customs, from strong Tex-Mex influences in Texas and Kansas to the quintessentially Canadian butter tarts among the Amish in Ontario, Canada.

Additionally, this book features fewer communities in the West and in Canada than in other places because these areas have a smaller Amish population. The American West will likely experience continued growth in their Amish numbers as their populations rise in eastern states. Colorado and Montana are leading the way with Amish settlers. But even in Montana, which has had an Amish presence since the mid-1970s, the total population of Old Order Amish numbers less than one thousand.

While we couldn't cover every Amish community in the United States, we hope this book will provide an interesting and exciting culinary and cultural journey into the kitchens of a diverse sampling of Amish cooks across America. We hope you enjoy discovering how very different these kitchens are, and trying a few of their recipes in your own kitchen.

PICTURING THE AMISH

In previous cookbooks in the Amish Cook series, we've spent the majority of our time at Lovina Eicher's house. I've enjoyed a lifelong rapport and relationship with the Eicher family, and with that comes a comfort level that has afforded us the opportunity to share some gorgeous and captivating images. The working conditions with this cookbook were starkly different. Photographer Rachel Diver Williams, who also happens to be my wife, did an excellent job of working in and with unfamiliar settings to create a beautiful photographic portrait of Amish cooks across America. Often we arrived in a settlement and had only a day or two to really build a rapport, take photos, and sample recipes before moving on to the next. But almost everyone was very gracious, and we made some lasting friendships from the journey.

Although the Old Order Amish are generally not the completely insular, agrarian people they once were, they are still by their nature pretty private. Most Amish have religious restrictions that prohibit them from being photographed. Some Amish are more accepting of photographs than others. Those who do object to photography on religious grounds often cite Exodus 20:4: "Thou shalt not make unto thee any graven image, or any likeness of anything that is in heaven above, or that is in the earth beneath, or that is in the water under the earth."

Not all Amish reject photography for religious reasons. Some object because they think photography is prideful or frivolous. Others don't object to photos, but they don't want other Amish to be offended or upset by their participation in photography. We experienced a variety of cultural conditions. On one end of the spectrum, the ultraconservative Swartzentruber Amish of Ethridge, Tennessee (see page 107), didn't even want photographs taken *outside* their homes. We proposed maybe photographing some food on a picnic table in

their yards, but even that idea was vetoed. In each case, we respectfully complied, no questions asked. This book was and is intended to be a cultural cookbook, and photos—or their absence—is part of that story. So the lack of photos in some sections speaks as much about local values as their inclusion in others. The Amish in the Conewango Valley of New York and in Beeville, Texas, objected to photos almost as much as did the Amish in Ethridge. On the other end of the spectrum, the Amish in Rexford and St. Ignatius, Montana, didn't object to being photographed so long as they weren't posing, a practice that they believe reflects vanity. In between, we had many Amish who didn't object to hands, feet, and shadows appearing in photos.

Because we wanted to capture an honest, authentic portrayal of Amish life, we didn't rearrange furniture and decor to fit some preconceived photo style. Some Amish homemakers greeted us with a flair that would make Martha Stewart pause with admiration, whereas others had a more laid-back approach to our visit. All of the on-location photos featured in this book offer unfiltered genuine glimpses into Amish life.

ANATOMY OF AN AMISH RECIPE

Throughout this book, most of the recipes are in the same format, with measurements conveniently listed, oven temperatures and baking times provided. But is this how the recipes looked when we obtained them? No way!

Amish cooks typically cook and bake from generational cues, using tips, hints, and recipes passed down through generations. Recipes are written on tattered note cards, scraps of paper, and frequently not at all. We often sat down at kitchen tables and coaxed recipes out of people. In a few cases, if Amish contributors were comfortable with the technology, I'd just bring my laptop into their living rooms and type as they talked. It made for an odd juxtaposition.

Most Amish cooks we met were eager to provide their recipes, though some expressed frustration at me wanting them to enunciate every step. "Oh, certainly anyone would know how much flour to add!" said one exasperated Amish cook. But most had a good sense of humor about it as we committed the recipes to writing. Once that was done, we had a team of volunteers waiting to test the recipes while I put them in the convenient format you see in this book. The two recipes that follow are very typical of the original format that we received. Often we'd have to test recipes with trial and error because once we left an Amish home, it'd be very difficult to reach someone for follow-up questions, as most didn't have telephones. The following recipes didn't make the final cut for other reasons, but see if you can play recipe editor and figure them out.

RAW VEGETABLE CASSEROLE
St. Ignatius, Montana (see page 157)

Fresh cabbage, coarsely cut

Potatoes, thickly sliced

Carrots

Onions

Salt

Pepper

In a roaster or baking dish, put a thick layer of fresh cabbage. Then layer the potatoes, carrots, and onions on top of the cabbage. Repeat the layers until the roaster is full. Use only cabbage on the bottom layer. Last over all, put a layer of raw meat, elk or hamburger. Cover tightly with a lid or foil. Bake 1½ to 2 hours. Before serving, cover with cheese slices. Other fresh vegetables could be used in season.

SWEET POTATO PIE
Pontotoc, Mississippi (see page 113)

1 large cup sweet potatoes

6 tablespoons flour

1½ cups sugar

½ cup brown sugar

5 eggs

Salt, cinnamon, and vanilla

Enough hot milk to make 3 pies (about 5½ cups)

Do not have the oven too hot.

AMISH COOKS ACROSS THE
EAST

Lured by William Penn's promise of religious freedom, the Amish first settled in Berks County, Pennsylvania, in 1740. Known as the Northkill settlement, this community established the Amish identity in the United States. Among the early settlers were Yoders, Troyers, Hostetlers, and Hershbergers, surnames that would become synonymous with being Amish in America over the centuries ahead. Northkill was largely frontier country, and life there was hardscrabble. Native American raids resulted in casualties and clashes, which caused the Amish to gradually fan out to other areas, usually gravitating to available farmland and to places where local laws assured them of religious freedom and where clashes with the natives would be minimal.

"Back then, the Amish weren't that much different than anyone else. Everyone dressed similarly and traveled by horse and buggy," said Kathryn Miller, an Amish woman who now lives in St. Ignatius, Montana, one of the farthest settlements from the Berks County beachhead. It would be almost two centuries before the Amish would settle that far west (see page 157). In the 1700s and early 1800s, the Amish settled first in other parts of Pennsylvania and then in Delaware, Maryland, and eventually points west.

Today, Pennsylvania is home to a varied Amish population, from enclaves of the most conservative Amish found around New Wilmington and in Mifflin County, to some of the most progressive Old Order Amish in Lancaster County. The Amish of Mifflin County are known as the Nebraska Amish (so named because an early faction of this sect lived for a time in the Cornhusker State) and are the most conservative Amish anywhere. Their followers usually wear only dark clothing, but their conservatism contrasts with some Old Order Amish in Lancaster County, who can be seen using motorized farm equipment and chatting on cell phones.

Around New Wilmington, Pennsylvania, buggy tops are a distinctive chocolate color, while elsewhere, they are yellow.

Eastern Amish settlements are home to such classic fare as shoofly pie and chicken-corn soup, but a wide variety of other foods can be found in other places. For example, apples are king in the lush Mohawk Valley of Upstate New York, homemade maple syrup infuses the baked goods in the Empire State's rural Conewango Valley, and blueberries and potatoes are a colorful yin and yang on the supper table in rural Maine. Some Amish even partake in moose hunts in the far north, enjoying game that their Midwestern counterparts could only imagine.

Because Pennsylvania's Amish population has saturated the state, the Amish are constantly in search of new places to settle. Upstate New York has seen the biggest boom in the "plain" population as Amish have settled in the Mohawk Valley and the state's rugged North Country. But the largest settlement of Amish in the East is in Lancaster, Pennsylvania. Such confections as shoofly pie and whoopie pies join such dishes as funnel cakes and homemade pretzels to make Lancaster Amish synonymous with hearty culinary traditions.

Heavily populated New England states—Connecticut, Vermont, Massachusetts, Rhode Island, and New Hampshire—do not have any Amish presence. However, as the Amish population grows, it is possible that rural areas of western Massachusetts and New Hampshire could prove appealing in the years ahead. Following are some tasty stops across the East.

CONEWANGO VALLEY • CHERRY CREEK, NEW YORK

AT A GLANCE

Date established: 1949

Number of church districts: 14

Culinary highlights: homemade maple syrup

Tucked away in the far southwestern corner of the Empire State lies a world far different from that of the gleaming Manhattan skyscrapers that most people associate with New York. There are no subways, checkered cabs, or trendy shops selling the latest fashions. This part of New York is marked by a quiet stillness that hangs over the hills. The Old Order Amish have farmed these valleys for generations, living off the land and scratching out a living in a variety of home-based businesses, including quilt shops, harness makers, fabric outlets, and furniture builders. An Amish candy shop and a toy store attract outsiders to this area, dubbed by local tourism officials as "New York's Amish Trail."

The Conewango Valley is home to New York State's oldest and largest Amish settlement, with fourteen sprawling Amish church districts. Because the settlement is so spread out geographically,

Amish parochial schools can be found on main roads every few miles, so no child has more than a 2-mile trek to class. On some snowy winter days, of which there are many in this lake-effect snow belt, Amish children can be seen getting to class in many manners: on foot, by sleigh, and sometimes even on cross-country skis.

While Upstate New York has experienced a surge in its Amish population over the past decade, Amish life in this western New York valley has continued as it has for more than half a century. The Amish here are steeped in traditions that define their day-to-day lives. Dutch boy haircuts for the men, bright blue doors, and some of the nation's finest homemade maple syrup distinguish this area from other Amish settlements. No one seems to know anymore why the doors are blue, but the tradition is adhered to and passed down from generation to generation.

"I just go to the hardware store and they'll do a color match of the blue paint that I want," explained Barbara Miller, who, along with her husband, runs an Amish bakery on Route 62 outside of Cherry Creek. The store features several bright blue entryways. The Miller bakery is known locally for its tire-size maple-dipped doughnuts, coffeecakes, whoopie pies, and other confections. Like many of the Amish businesses in the area, the bakery doesn't have a name. "Oh, we're just called the 'bakery on Route 62,'" Barbara said matter-of-factly when asked what her business's name was.

The spring and summer seasons bring plenty of tourists into the area, many stopping by the bakery for one of Barbara's doughnuts. But a second busy season occurs at the bakery in the weeks prior to Thanksgiving, when her pies are the prize.

"Before Thanksgiving we have people from as far away as Buffalo coming to buy our pies," Barbara said as she sat in a hickory rocker, dressed in typical plain attire of head covering and plain blue dress.

Perhaps no other Amish area is as synonymous with syrup as the Conewango Valley. The silver buckets that appear on sugar

maple trees are a familiar sight in Amish yards through the area each March. Those trees are found in lush abundance in this region. As winter begins to loosen its icy grip each year, the sap begins its ebb and flow deep within the tree trunks. As sure as tulips and crocuses begin to bloom, so, too, do maple syrup buckets. Many Amish homeowners in the valley tap their trees to savor the sugary sweetness of the earth. Drive the grid of rural roads in the area on crisp late winter days and you're likely to see steam rising from a "sugar shack," a specially built building used just for sugaring that often sits back from the main house.

The sap is harvested, boiled down, and made into maple syrup that then finds its way into Amish-made cakes, puddings, breads, and candies. Some Amish in the area actually drink the sap straight from the tree, and some claim therapeutic benefits from drinking straight sap. It pours like water, not like the thick, sugary liquid it can become, and it tastes like a smooth, slightly sweetened water.

At the Yost Miller farmstead, spring is a busy time for making maple syrup. The Millers put out more than four hundred buckets each spring and gather the sap in 5-gallon metal pails before it's transported to a holding container to await boiling. The Millers boil their sap in their kitchen, forgoing the amenity of a sugar shack.

Yost Miller bottles several kinds of syrup, depending on the climate conditions. The earlier sap produces a lighter syrup. Miller knows the syrup well. They are categorized as "Grade A" and "Grade B." Grade A syrup is further divided into "light amber" and "dark amber." Grade B is the darkest, thickest, most maple-infused syrup, making it best for baking. The Grade B syrup tends to come at the end of sugaring season, when the warmth begins to surge the sap.

"The darker it is, the stronger it tastes," Miller said of the syrup.

In the Conewango Valley, you can find plenty of Amish selling maple syrup, though fewer are making it these days. Throughout syrup season, you'll always find small hand-scrawled signs at the ends of driveways advertising homemade maple syrup for sale, especially when you drive the back roads of the valley. The Amish entrepreneurs often offer the pricey delicacy in different-size bottles to fit different budgets and needs.

On my visit to the Conewango Valley during a sugaring season, an Amish man, bundled against the New York chill, was securing what looked like a sap collection tank. I explained to the gentleman what I was doing and that I'd love to watch the syrup-making firsthand. He was affable and relatively enthusiastic about the visit, and he said to come back the next morning to watch him and his sons make the syrup.

However, his enthusiasm wasn't shared by the Amish woman, presumably his wife, who answered the door the next morning with a frosty look on her face. Not only that, but the weather was wrong. A late-season snow had fallen overnight, covering the valley in a fluffy overcoat of white.

"It was too cold for them to collect this morning," the woman said crisply, a few locks of white hair peeking out from beneath her *kapp*.

"Oh, that's too bad. Well, maybe I could just see the inside of the sugar shack just to get a feel for what it looks like?"

The woman stared silently.

"Or, maybe not. . . . Well, would it be okay to get a shot of the shack from the outside?"

She remained silent.

"From the outside—really far away, from the driveway as I'm leaving?" I asked.

"I think that would be okay," she finally said.

Done. Yes, I was disappointed at not seeing the sugaring and the woman not being more welcoming. But this Amish settlement is more conservative than some, and the woman was simply maintaining the generations-old insular traditions of the Amish. Some other Amish in the area were more receptive, and they explained that the uses for maple syrup in the Conewango Valley are as varied as the syrups themselves.

"We use maple syrup when canning peaches. Fill the jars with two-thirds maple syrup and the rest of the jar with water," Yost Miller explained. The Millers, like many of the Conewango Valley Amish, use fresh maple syrup in place of almost anything that requires sugar, from cookies and cakes to cereal.

Ben Shetler's family puts out more than one thousand buckets on their 40 acres. He stressed the importance of processing the sap quickly.

"If the sap runs today, you have to get to it tomorrow or it'll go sour on you," Shetler said.

The recipes that follow are among the mouth-watering maple favorites from the Conewango community.

HOMEMADE MAPLE CREAM
Makes about 2 pounds

This is a homemade concoction that is a favorite of many maple-syrup-producing families in the Conewango Valley. This is a tricky recipe whose success often depends on very slight variables in weather and syrup quality. The result should be a sweet spread that can be used like peanut butter. It tastes good just spread on toast.

4 cups pure maple syrup
   (Grade A light amber or medium amber work best)
5 drops vegetable oil or melted butter

Start by filling with very cold water either the sink or a pan larger than the one you'll use to make the maple cream. This will serve as a water bath. Have a candy thermometer handy. Partially fill with water a deep pan in which you'll make the maple cream.

Place the maple syrup in the latter pan (the boiling syrup will foam up fairly high when boiling). Add the 5 drops of oil to the maple syrup. This helps keep the foam down.

Boil over high heat without stirring until the temperature of the boiling syrup is 236°F. The syrup will get hot very quickly, so watch it carefully. The syrup can scorch or even catch fire if it cooks too long.

Remove the syrup from the heat and immediately place the pan in the water bath. Do not move, stir, or disturb the syrup while it cools. You may gently add some ice cubes to the water bath, if needed.

Let the hot syrup cool to room temperature. When you can hold the back of your hand close to the surface of the syrup and not feel heat radiating off the surface, it has cooled sufficiently.

Remove the pan from the water bath, and slowly stir the syrup with a wooden spoon until it loses its gloss and starts to become opaque. Its color will lighten, and you will be unable to see through it. Continue stirring until the syrup has the consistency of peanut butter. Spoon into containers and keep refrigerated. Use as a spread on toast or as a sweetener in recipes.

Alternate method: Pour the cooled maple syrup into the bowl of a stand mixer. Using a paddle blade, stir the syrup until it has the consistency of peanut butter and has become opaque. This can take up to 1 hour.

MAPLE-CINNAMON STICKY BUNS

Makes 12 rolls

These cinnamon rolls, infused with the fresh taste of maple, are a favorite in the Conewango Valley. The end-of-season, dark, Grade B maple syrup makes for the strongest maple taste, but any grade of syrup can be used in these rolls.

DOUGH

1½ cups warm (115°F) water

1 tablespoon plus 2 teaspoons
(0.65 ounces) active dry yeast

⅓ cup granulated sugar

4½ to 5 cups all-purpose flour

⅓ cup vegetable oil

½ teaspoon salt

1 large egg, beaten

2 tablespoons pure maple syrup

SYRUP

4½ tablespoons unsalted butter,
plus some for greasing a pan

½ cup pure maple syrup

½ cup firmly packed light brown sugar

FILLING

3 tablespoons butter, softened

½ cup firmly packed light brown sugar

2 teaspoons ground cinnamon

2 tablespoons pure maple syrup

Continued

Make the dough: Pour the warm water into a large mixing bowl. Sprinkle the yeast and sugar into the water. Stir and let it stand until foamy, at least 3 minutes. When the yeast is foamy, mix in 1 cup of the flour until incorporated. Add the oil, salt, egg, and maple syrup. Add just enough flour that the dough is no longer sticky. It should take about 3½ more cups, but you may need more or less. Mix with a dough hook attached to a mixer on medium speed for 2 to 3 minutes, or knead by hand for 3 to 5 minutes. Place in a greased bowl, cover with plastic wrap, and let rise in a warm place for about 1 hour.

Make the syrup: Grease a 19 by 13-inch baking pan. Combine the maple syrup and butter in a small saucepan over medium heat and stir until the butter melts. Remove the saucepan from the heat. Mix in the brown sugar. Pour the syrup into the prepared baking pan, and tilt the pan to evenly coat the bottom.

Punch down the dough, and roll it on a well-floured surface into a 13 by 18-inch rectangle about ¼ inch thick. Preheat the oven to 350°F.

Make the filling: Spread the softened butter all over the rectangle, except for a narrow butter-free strip along one of the long edges. In a medium bowl, combine the brown sugar and cinnamon. Spread the cinnamon-sugar mixture over the dough, gently pressing, until evenly distributed. Drizzle the maple syrup over the filling. Starting with the buttered long edge, roll up the dough and pinch the edges to secure. Cut the dough with a sharp, serrated knife into twelve equal pieces. Place in the prepared baking pan. Cover and let the rolls rise for 30 to 45 minutes, until puffy.

Bake for 20 to 25 minutes, until light golden brown. Remove from the oven, immediately invert onto a baking sheet, and let cool for 5 minutes. Serve warm.

HOMEMADE MAPLE SYRUP COOKIES
Makes about 4 dozen cookies

These cookies are faintly sweet with just a hint of maple flavor. Additional maple syrup could be used for a stronger maple taste. This is a soft cookie that can be enjoyed with a cup of coffee for breakfast.

1 teaspoon baking soda

1 tablespoon milk

1 large egg, beaten

½ cup shortening

1 cup pure maple syrup

3 cups all-purpose flour

1 tablespoon baking powder

½ teaspoon salt

1 teaspoon vanilla extract

Preheat the oven to 350°F.

Dissolve the baking soda in the milk in a small bowl, and set aside. In a large bowl, mix the egg, shortening, syrup, flour, baking powder, salt, and vanilla, in that order, until fully combined. The dough will be very thick and sticky. Add the soda mixture, and mix until fully incorporated.

Drop the dough by rounded teaspoonfuls 2 inches apart on an ungreased baking sheet. Bake until the cookies look set and are honey brown, 10 to 12 minutes. Let the cookies cool for a couple of minutes, then remove them from the baking sheet. The cookies will remain soft when stored in an airtight container.

MALINDA'S CANDY SHOP

Malinda Miller started selling baked goods to the public, but when she realized how quickly they would deteriorate, she switched to candy and confections that she'd make in her mother's kitchen. That was in 1995. Now, she has her own store on a rural road outside of Cherry Creek. The isolation doesn't scare away customers, who come from all over to stock up on her homemade and handmade candies, such as chocolate-covered cashew crunch and goat-milk fudge. She also offers an assortment of homemade jellies and jams reflecting local flavors. Elderberry, raspberry, strawberry-rhubarb, and blackberry are among the homemade jam flavors popular at Malinda's.

"Christmas and Easter are our busiest seasons," Malinda said, surveying pieces of parchment paper filled end to end with just-decorated chocolate bunnies.

Malinda's shop is tucked away in a tiny building in front of a well-kept home and is a popular stop along the Amish Trail.

RENSSELAER FALLS, NEW YORK

AT A GLANCE

Date established: 1992

Number of church districts: 2

Culinary highlights: elderberries, homemade bean soup

Northern New York is practically a state within a state. Locals affectionately call their slice of paradise the "North Country," a land of rugged, aging mountains, crisp creeks, and meandering moose. It wasn't until after the year 2000 that the Amish population really took root in the area.

According to Anna Miller, an Old Order Amish resident of the community, elderberries grow thick and wild, especially along fence rows. Locals eagerly cultivate the berries and make them into pies, jams, and coffeecakes. Thick soups like the one in this chapter help while away the winter.

YANKEE OR ENGLISH?

The Amish often refer to non-Amish outsiders as "English." This terminology dates back to the early American colonial times, when the Amish spoke German as their first language (as they still do today) and English was becoming the dominant language in the early states. So the Amish began referring to anyone who wasn't Amish as "English." Another term that was used to differentiate Amish from non-Amish was "Yankee." That term still is used often by older Amish but seems to be gradually falling by the wayside.

Randy James, in his book *Why Cows Learn Dutch*, said the term "Yankee" does not have Civil War roots, as the term might imply; rather, that the Amish used the expression to refer to someone who has left the Amish faith. Someone was "yanked over" was a common expression. According to James, the term was traditionally most popular in the Geauga County, Ohio, Amish settlement (one of the largest in the world), but whether the Amish or the Yankees coined the term has been lost to history. Amish who moved elsewhere took the term with them, and it gradually became a catchall phrase for anyone who wasn't Amish.

YANKEE BEAN SOUP
Makes 4 to 6 servings

This is a thick, hearty soup that has a little bit of everything in it. Such soups are mainstays through the harsh New England winters. The molasses balances out the savory for an excellent meal. A thick piece of crusty bread goes good with this soup.

1¼ cups dried navy beans, rinsed and cleaned

5 cups water

1 teaspoon molasses

½ cup diced salt pork

⅓ cup finely chopped celery leaves

½ teaspoon salt, plus extra for seasoning

3 strips fresh bacon, cut into small pieces

¼ cup finely chopped onion

½ cup diced, cooked carrots

2 cups milk

Place the beans in 4- or 5-quart saucepan or Dutch oven, add the water, and bring to a boil. Remove the pot from the heat, and let it stand, covered, for 2 to 24 hours. (The longer the beans soak, the softer the finished beans and the thicker the broth.)

Add the molasses, salt pork, celery leaves, and ½ teaspoon of salt. Cover the pot, and simmer for 2 hours, or until the beans are tender. Shake the pan or stir occasionally to prevent sticking.

While the soup is simmering, cook the bacon pieces and onion in a small skillet until the bacon is lightly browned. Mash the beans slightly. Add the bacon, onion, carrots, and milk to the beans. Season with additional salt. Cover and simmer the soup for 10 minutes more. The soup is then ready to serve or can be cooked longer to the desired consistency.

ELDERBERRY CUSTARD PIE

Makes one 9-inch pie

Elderberries are typically harvested in late summer in the northeastern United States. Some Amish claim medicinal benefits from elderberries.

1 cup elderberry juice

¼ cup all-purpose flour

1 cup sugar

¼ teaspoon salt

1 large egg, separated

1 cup milk

1 (9-inch) unbaked pie shell

Preheat the oven to 350°F.

Bring the juice to a boil over medium heat in a medium saucepan. While it's heating, combine the flour, sugar, and salt in a small mixing bowl, and gradually add the egg yolk and milk. Add to the boiling juice and stir until thickened. Remove the mixture from the heat.

Beat the egg white with a whisk or hand mixer in a medium mixing bowl until stiff peaks form. Fold the beaten egg white into the elderberry mixture until evenly combined. Pour the filling into the pie shell. Bake for 20 to 30 minutes, until the center is bubbly.

UNITY, MAINE

AT A GLANCE

Date established: 2008

Number of church districts: 1

Culinary highlights: blueberries, potatoes

Just outside the town of Unity, a motorist might notice a yellow caution sign warning of horse-and-buggy traffic. It's a sign of an unlikely Amish settlement that's tucked away among the rocky, rambling blueberry patches of central Maine. Unity is only about 25 miles, as the crow flies, from the postcard scenes of Maine's coast.

Maine has not been a traditional Amish stronghold, but that is changing. Since the 1700s, the state has been home to the last practicing community of Shakers in the United States at Sabbathday Lake. While there are similarities with simplicity and cuisine, Shakers evolved from a completely different religious movement.

The Unity settlement is known in Amish parlance as a "daughter settlement." This means that there is no bishop in the community. Unity is a daughter of the more established Maine Amish community of Smyrna, about an hour to the northeast. The bishop in Smyrna oversees the activities of the church in Unity and visits several times a year to preside over communion and other formal functions. When the settlement reaches about twenty-five families, Unity will have its own bishop installed and then another daughter settlement will be started. In this way the Amish communities are "planted" singularly in scattered areas, as opposed to being clustered.

The Unity community maintains close ties with the community in Aylmer, Ontario (see page 22). Church members often hire a

driver and complete the 12-hour journey to Aylmer, crossing into Quebec en route to Ontario through the sparsely populated Maine town of Coburn Gore. The Amish in Unity maintain deep family, traditional, and theological ties with Aylmer, so journeys between the two outposts are common and important.

Several characteristics of the Amish who live in Unity are distinct. While the Amish traditionally don't evangelize, some settlements—Unity among them—like to act as a "beacon" for others. Although they aren't necessarily seeking converts, they *are* seeking to share their message with others.

Across the country, the typical Amish church service is held in a home. The Amish in Unity worship in a separate building. Another of the few exceptions is the settlement in Pinecraft, Florida; see page 126. Church members have just completed a "meetinghouse," where meals and fellowship can be found after church. The meals are eaten cafeteria style, the men seated on one side of the room, the women on the other. Sandwiches, homemade bars, and cookies are popular items served after church.

Another unique characteristic of note concerns facial hair. A visitor to amishcookonline.com once posted a photo from the Waterville, Maine, newspaper of an Amish farmer out in the fields plowing. What was unusual about the photograph is that it showed a mustachioed Amish man. The photo sparked a lot of discussion on the website, with one posting going especially far: "I doubt if the photo was of an Amish man at all, the fellow is probably a local back-to-nature homesteader who has ties to the Amish community."

Turns out the photo was of Unity resident Abner Stoll, who is very much Old Order Amish.

"There was a lot of buzz about that mustache of yours," a visitor said to Abner over lunch, during a visit to Unity. "Some people suggested you probably aren't even Amish."

He just laughed and brushed off the comments. The Old Order Amish have historically eschewed mustaches because of the belief that they were militaristic symbols of some sort. The Stolls and others in this Maine church district don't share that interpretation of the mustache. He explained that they didn't associate the mustache with anything militaristic, but that they didn't look down upon other Amish who did.

Resident Elizabeth Stoll's tidy home sits on 200 acres of wooded hills atop a bluff overlooking the pastoral Maine countryside. Far to the north, Mount Katahdin catches the first rays of sunlight in the United States each day. Off to the east, Cadillac Mountain serves as the highest point on the eastern seaboard.

Elizabeth, who is Abner Stoll's mother, has lived in many places over many years: Ohio; Arkansas; Tennessee; Alymer, Ontario (see page 22); and now Maine. "Home is where the children are," she said. Four of her seven children live in the community.

After a lunch of fresh tomato and cheese sandwiches, potatoes fried in a cast-iron skillet, and corn grown in the rocky Maine soil, I visited the Community Market, the general store operated by Elizabeth's son Caleb. It has been a boon to the rural residents in the area, Amish and non-Amish alike, selling bulk food and hardware. One of Caleb Stoll's daughters thought it would be fun to make fresh doughnuts to sell to customers, and Elizabeth Stoll's youngest son, Abner, sort of took on the project. So he oversees the preparation

and sale of the doughnuts, and the general store became known as much for its fresh doughnuts as for its fertilizer and wrenches.

"There's just something about a freshly made doughnut that really is popular with customers," Caleb Stoll explains of the glazed doughnuts, which are sold only on Wednesday mornings, 350 to 400 in a typical week. "The doughnuts just really took off."

Late summer is prime blueberry time in central Maine. The fields are full of plump, flavorful azure globes. Most of the blueberries harvested in the Unity area are low bush or high bush, which aren't really all that high. Although the high-bush variety is cultivated, the low bushes are grown wild, not picked by hand but harvested using a device that Elizabeth describes as looking a bit like a dustpan with prongs on it. After the berries are harvested, they are put through a winnowing machine to clean out any debris or dirt. The high-bush blueberries are picked by hand. When blueberries begin to come into season, baked goods among Unity Amish become infused with them. Jams, muffins, coffeecakes, and breads begin to burst with blue.

Another Maine crop: potatoes. Homemade potato soup is another favorite in Unity, and Elizabeth Stoll can often be found frying potatoes in her late mother's cast-iron skillet.

Elizabeth shared some of her favorite blueberry and potato recipes.

MELT-IN-YOUR-MOUTH BLUEBERRY CAKE
Serves 8 to 12

As the name implies, this is a soft cake. A favorite way for the Amish in this area to enjoy the cake is to crumble it into a bowl and pour milk over it.

1½ cups fresh blueberries, rinsed and picked clean

1½ cups sifted all-purpose flour

2 large eggs, separated

1¼ cups sugar

½ cup shortening

¼ teaspoon salt

1 teaspoon vanilla extract

1 teaspoon baking powder

⅓ cup milk

Preheat the oven to 350°F. Grease an 8 by 8-inch baking pan and set aside.

Gently shake the blueberries in a small amount of the flour in a large bowl, and set aside. This will help prevent their sinking in the finished cake.

Beat the egg whites in a large bowl, slowly adding ¼ cup of the sugar, until stiff peaks form. Set aside. In a separate bowl, cream the shortening, and add the salt and vanilla. Add the remaining 1 cup of sugar (reserve 1 tablespoon) and the egg yolks, and beat until light and creamy. Sift together the remaining sifted flour and the baking powder into another bowl. Add the dry ingredients, alternately with the milk, to the creamed mixture until evenly incorporated.

Fold in the beaten whites, then fold in the blueberries. Pour the batter into the prepared baking pan, and sprinkle the top with the remaining tablespoon of granulated sugar. Bake for 1 hour, or until a toothpick inserted into the center comes out clean.

BLUEBERRY-LEMON BUTTERMILK MUFFINS
Makes 24 muffins

The lemon adds a tang to the sweetness of the blueberries, making for a burst of flavors. Locally grown and harvested blueberries give these muffins a very fresh taste.

3 cups all-purpose flour

2 teaspoons baking powder

1 teaspoon baking soda

½ teaspoon salt

1 cup (2 sticks) butter, softened

1½ cups sugar

4 large eggs

2½ tablespoons fresh lemon juice

2 tablespoons lemon zest (see Note)

1 teaspoon vanilla extract

1 cup buttermilk

2 cups fresh blueberries

GLAZE

1½ cups powdered sugar

3 tablespoons fresh lemon juice

1 tablespoon lemon zest (see Note)

Preheat the oven to 350°F. Lightly grease two standard muffin pans, or line the pans with cupcake papers.

In a large mixing bowl, combine the flour, baking powder, baking soda, and salt. Set aside.

In a medium mixing bowl, cream the butter and sugar. Beat in the eggs, one at a time. Add the lemon juice, lemon zest, and vanilla and combine until smooth. Beat in the flour mixture and buttermilk, alternating the two, using about one-third of each for each addition. The mixture should be smooth and creamy. Fold in the blueberries, and mix until they are evenly distributed throughout the batter. Pour the batter into the muffin pans, filling each cup about halfway.

Bake until the muffin tops are golden, 20 to 25 minutes. Allow to cool for about 5 minutes.

Make the glaze: Stir the powdered sugar, lemon juice, and lemon zest until smooth. Brush the glaze over the muffin tops while the muffins are still warm.

Note: Both the batter and the glaze use the juice and zest of lemons, so be sure to zest the lemons before extracting the juice.

BLUEBERRY-FILLED COFFEECAKE
Serves 8 to 12

This classic coffeecake is a favorite during blueberry season. Other fruits could be substituted for the blueberries when available.

BATTER

½ cup (1 stick) butter, softened

½ cup sugar

1 large egg

1½ cups all-purpose flour

½ teaspoon salt

1½ teaspoons baking powder

½ teaspoon vanilla extract

½ cup milk

1 (16-ounce) can blueberry pie filling

TOPPING

¼ cup firmly packed brown sugar

¼ cup all-purpose flour

2 tablespoons butter, softened

¼ cup chopped walnuts

Preheat the oven to 350°F. Grease an 8 by 8-inch baking pan.

Make the batter: Cream the butter and sugar together in a small mixing bowl until smooth. Add the egg and beat until well combined. Add the flour, salt, baking powder, vanilla, and milk and mix until smooth. The batter will be thick—the consistency of cookie dough. Spread half the batter into the prepared pan. Spoon the pie filling over the batter, then cover with the remaining batter.

Make the topping: Thoroughly mix the topping ingredients in a small mixing bowl until they form the consistency of coarse sand. Sprinkle the topping crumbs on top of the batter in the pan, and bake for 40 minutes, or until the top is golden brown.

POTATO SUPREME
Serves 8 to 10

With this dish, the potatoes turn brown very quickly after peeling and/or grating. It is best to have the rest of your casserole assembled, then quickly add the peeled and grated potatoes to avoid having a gray-looking potato dish.

SAUCE

4 tablespoons (½ stick) butter

¼ cup all-purpose flour

2 cups milk

POTATOES

1½ cups (3 sticks) melted butter

½ cup chopped onion

¼ teaspoon black pepper

4 ounces cream cheese, softened

1 teaspoon salt

2 pounds potatoes, peeled and grated

TOPPING

2 cups cornflakes, crushed

4 tablespoons (½ stick) butter, melted

1 teaspoon dried parsley (optional)

Preheat the oven to 350°F.

Make the sauce: Melt the butter in a medium saucepan over medium heat. Whisk in the flour to form a paste. Gradually add the milk, whisking constantly. Cook until the mixture thickens into a smooth sauce.

Make the potato mixture: Place the sauce in a large bowl. Add the melted butter, onion, pepper, cream cheese, and salt, and combine thoroughly. Stir in the potatoes and mix thoroughly. Pour the potato mixture into a 2-quart casserole dish.

Make the topping: Combine the cornflakes, melted butter, and parsley flakes, and sprinkle on top of the assembled casserole. Bake for 1½ hours, or until the top of the casserole is golden brown and crisp.

Note: For a heartier casserole, brown 1 pound of ground beef or sausage, and stir the browned meat into the potato mixture before transferring to a 4-quart casserole dish.

POTATO CHOWDER
Serves 4 to 6

Chowders are a staple of Maine menus, and the Amish contribute to that popularity. True to a chowder, this is a thick, creamy concoction using fresh, locally grown Maine potatoes.

2 tablespoons butter

1 small onion, chopped

3 cups chicken broth

3 medium-size potatoes, peeled and cut into medium dice

3 medium carrots, peeled and cut into medium dice

2 tablespoons dried parsley

½ teaspoon salt

½ teaspoon black pepper

¼ cup all-purpose flour

1 cup milk

8 ounces cream cheese, at room temperature, or 4 ounces softened cream cheese plus 4 ounces shredded Cheddar

2 large chicken breast halves, cooked and cut into medium dice (about 2 cups)

Melt the butter in a small saucepan over low heat. Add the onion and cook until soft, about 5 minutes. Add the chicken broth, potatoes, and carrots. Bring to a boil, then decrease the heat and simmer until the potatoes and carrots are fork-tender, about 20 minutes. Add the parsley flakes, salt, and pepper.

Stir the flour and milk together in a small bowl until smooth, add the flour mixture to the soup, and bring the soup to a boil. Stir the soup until it begins to thicken. Add the cheese and mix until the cheese has melted into the soup. Stir in the chicken, and continue cooking until the chicken is heated through, but do not boil.

THE AMISH COOK'S EASTERN OBSERVATIONS

BY LOVINA EICHER

I am familiar with many of the foods out east: Blueberries, potatoes, and rhubarb are enjoyed around here, too.

The wedding cakes in Fredonia, Pennsylvania, are different than what I was used to growing up. In some Amish areas you are not allowed to have tiered cakes. In Berne they were a little pickier about not having wedding cakes too fancy.

The rhubarb juice in the Fredonia chapter is not something I had ever tried until I moved to Michigan. It was interesting to hear about all the different kinds of apples in the Lyndonville community. Some of those varieties are ones I want to try!

 ## AMISH COOKS ACROSS CANADA

AYLMER, ONTARIO

AT A GLANCE

Date established: 1953

Number of church districts: 3

Culinary highlights: butter tarts

This part of Ontario is sometimes known as the "banana belt." It's a tongue-in-cheek moniker. There are no bananas grown here, but the nickname stems from Aylmer's location near the southernmost point of the entire, sprawling country. The southern Ontario climate is typically temperate, and winters, surprising to people in the United States, aren't very snowy.

Canada has always embraced its multiculturalism. From Acadians in the Maritimes to French in Quebec to Inuits in the North and Native Americans in the West, Canada is a diverse cultural cauldron. So it's no surprise that Canada's Amish communities are tinged with the same diverse blush as the rest of the country. And perhaps nowhere is this "plain ethnicity" more in evidence than Aylmer, Ontario. In this tiny town of 7,500 people is a diverse settlement of Russian Mennonites, Mexican Mennonites, and traditional Old Order Amish.

The first "plain presence" in the Aylmer area took root in 1953, when several Amish families from Ohio bought farms in the area. They were leaving Pike County, Ohio, after it was announced that a nuclear enrichment facility was going to be built there. The pacifist Amish weren't happy about having such an important cog of a war machine in their backyards and dreaded the increased traffic the plant would bring to their quiet Ohio redoubt. Another enticement Aylmer offered was being in Canada, which was not involved in the Korean War at the time. While young Amish men could claim conscientious objector status to avoid the war in the United States, they were still drafted to service in hospitals and factories to help the war effort on the home front.

Now there are three church districts that call this charming community home. Since those first Amish families arrived—among them the Stolls (see page 15)—Aylmer has become an important Amish settlement.

Aylmer is a quintessentially Canadian village with a bustling downtown. Amish shoppers carry reusable shopping bags, partly a reflection of the community's ecological awareness, partly a reaction to Ontario's plastic bag tax.

Some refer to Aylmer as the intellectual capital of the Amish. The Heritage Historical Library is here and it is home to some towering figures within the Amish church. It is also the home of Pathway Publishing, a publishing house owned and operated entirely by Old Order Amish.

Pathway Publishing was founded in 1964 by two Amish farmers, Joseph Stoll and David Wagler. It has since grown to include fifteen employees, two book fulfillment warehouses, and scores of new titles each year, including a wide variety of fiction and nonfiction books and magazines, *Family Life*, *Young Companion*, and *Blackboard Bulletin*. Although they wouldn't be mistaken by anyone for *Vogue* or *Vanity Fair*, *Family Life* and *Young Companion* are staples in almost every Amish household across America. *Blackboard Bulletin* is published for parochial schoolteachers to catch up on the latest texts and trends in education. Typed on manual typewriters and then printed on diesel-powered printers in standard black ink on white paper, the magazines offer an assortment of advice, tips, and spiritual guidance to living simply.

"People in Aylmer have come from everywhere, so the food is different from household to household," said one Amish man. So borscht competes for menu space alongside tortillas and shoofly pie. But one food that everyone seems to share is the tart. Butter tarts are a purely Canadian creation and the Amish have embraced them, filling them with raisins, apples, or coconut.

NEVER-FAIL PASTRY

Makes two 9-inch piecrusts

This is a popular piecrust recipe in many Amish settlements. This recipe is used to make a small pastry shell for the butter tarts that follow, but it can also be used to make two 9-inch piecrusts for any pie recipe in this book. Butter can be substituted for the lard.

2½ cups all-purpose flour

½ teaspoon salt

8 ounces lard

1 large egg

1 tablespoon vinegar

4 to 5 tablespoons very cold water

Stir the flour and salt together in a medium bowl. Cut in the lard with a pastry blender until it forms the consistency of oatmeal. In a cup, beat the egg lightly. To the egg, add the vinegar and water and stir until well beaten. Gradually add the egg mixture to the flour mixture, constantly stirring with a fork or knife until the dough holds together. The dough is ready to roll out and use for butter tarts or pies.

BUTTER TARTS
Makes about 20 tarts

Tarts are a quintessentially Canadian confection. You'll not find these sweet treats on any Amish menus south of the Canadian border. While the texture and taste can resemble that of a pecan pie, the lack of a thickener added makes the filling a little runnier. When combined with a crisp crust, the two contrasts make for great balance. The recipe allows for some optional additions such as raisins or coconuts, but many enjoy butter tarts without those.

1 recipe Never-Fail Pastry (page 24)

4 large eggs

½ cup firmly packed brown sugar

2 cups dark corn syrup

2 teaspoons vanilla extract

1 teaspoon white vinegar

10 tablespoons butter, softened

2 cups raisins, walnuts, or coconut (optional)

Preheat the oven to 350°F. Lightly grease about 20 standard muffin cups.

Roll out the pastry dough on a lightly floured surface to form a 12-inch-diameter circle. Use a glass to cut out rounds and place them in the muffin pans. Cut off any excess overhang.

In a large mixing bowl, combine the eggs, brown sugar, corn syrup, vanilla, vinegar, and butter and beat until the mixture is creamy and thoroughly mixed.

Spoon the optional ingredients into the bottom of the unfilled crusts. Pour the combined mixture into the pastry crusts until three-quarters full. Bake until the crusts are golden and the filling is firm.

FREDONIA, PENNSYLVANIA

AT A GLANCE

Date established: 1990

Number of church districts: 2

Culinary highlights: rhubarb

Amish settlements of all sizes can be found spread across the Keystone State. Yes, Pennsylvania Amish almost always make people think of Lancaster County and its bustling Amish communities near Bird-in-Hand and Intercourse. But of the sixty thousand Amish who live in Pennsylvania, only about one-third of them live in Lancaster County. This leaves the rest of vast Pennsylvania as home to other Amish, in small and sprawling settlements.

Two church districts call the gentle hills outside of Fredonia home. Gravel roads unfurl like silver ribbon past tidy, well-tended homes. One of the homes belongs to Alva and Miriam Miller.

The settlement began in 1990 by Alva's late husband, Mahlon, who was looking to his more rural roots. They moved from a settlement in Ohio that allowed gasoline-powered tractors. Mahlon wanted to live in a community where farming was still practiced by horse-drawn plow. Word of mouth and a pleasant climate have helped Mahlon's vision come to fruition. More than twenty years later, the Amish outside Fredonia have grown to two church districts of more than forty families. Amish have moved to Fredonia from Kentucky, Ohio, Michigan, other parts of Pennsylvania, Delaware, and West Virginia.

Miriam Miller, one of Alva and Mahlon's daughters, is a bit of a renaissance woman. She teaches school, paints, writes, and bakes. What she has really become known for in her community, however, is delicious and decorative homemade wedding cakes. Miriam started playing with a cake-decorating kit her mother got when she was younger, and everything just sort of took off from there.

"My younger brother asked me to do his wedding cake, and then other people started asking me to do theirs," Miriam remembered.

She uses boxed mixes for the cake and then creates a delicious homemade icing using shortening, powdered sugar, water, salt, vanilla, butter, and flour. White cake with nuts and butter pecan are the two favorite wedding cake flavors in the Fredonia community, and "at a lot of the Amish weddings," Miriam noted, "the cake is served to the helpers." As in many Amish settlements, weddings are usually held on Thursdays. May and June are heavily favored in Fredonia, as are autumn weddings.

The Millers have a tidy garden with a row of rhubarb, and the western Pennsylvania soil helps nurture a monster crop. They have it well into the scorching summer, long after rhubarb patches elsewhere have withered. In a single day one spring, the family harvested 300 pounds from their row. Typically, rhubarb might be found in a jam or cobbler, but in Fredonia, rhubarb is enjoyed in breads, cookies, cakes, and even tapioca. Here, courtesy of Miriam Miller, are a few of the recipes, most of which make generous use of Fredonia's rhubarb.

RHUBARB BREAD

Makes 1 loaf

This is a nice bread just to slice and eat, similar to a pumpkin bread. It is wonderful as a breakfast bread and goes great with a glass of cold homemade rhubarb juice. Store leftover bread in a sealed bag. Leftover bread freezes well.

½ cup (1 stick) butter, softened

1 cup sugar

2 large eggs, beaten

2 tablespoons milk

2 cups all-purpose flour

½ teaspoon salt

1 teaspoon baking soda

1 teaspoon vanilla extract

1 cup cooked diced rhubarb, still hot

TOPPING

1 tablespoon butter, melted

1 tablespoon all-purpose flour

1 teaspoon hot water

1 tablespoon sugar

1 teaspoon ground cinnamon

Preheat the oven to 375°F. Lightly grease and flour a 5 by 9-inch loaf pan and set aside.

In a medium mixing bowl, cream the butter and sugar together until it becomes light and creamy. Add the eggs and milk, and mix well. In a small mixing bowl, sift together the flour, salt, and baking soda. Add this to the butter mixture, and stir until all the ingredients are thoroughly combined. Stir in the vanilla and hot rhubarb and mix until well combined. Pour the batter into the prepared pan.

Make the topping: In a small mixing bowl, combine the butter, flour, water, sugar, and cinnamon. Use a pastry blender to mix the ingredients thoroughly. Pour the mixture over the bread batter. Bake for 1 hour, or until a toothpick inserted into the center comes out clean. Let cool for 10 minutes in the loaf pan, then place the loaf on a wire rack. Slice, and eat either warm or cool.

RHUBARB STREUSEL CAKE
Serves 14 to 16

This cake tastes great with a scoop of cold vanilla ice cream on top. It resembles a coffeecake, and it's great at breakfast with a cup of coffee.

¾ cup sugar

4 tablespoons (½ stick) butter, softened

1 large egg, beaten

1 cup milk

2 cups all-purpose flour

1 teaspoon salt

2 teaspoons baking powder

1 pound rhubarb, cut into ¼-inch
 pieces (about 4 cups)

3 tablespoons strawberry-flavored
 gelatin, such as Jell-O

TOPPING

¾ cup sugar

½ cup all-purpose flour

½ cup quick-cooking oats

4 tablespoons (½ stick) butter

Whipped cream, for topping (optional)

Preheat the oven to 350°F. Lightly grease a 9 by 13-inch pan, and set aside.

In a large mixing bowl, combine the sugar and butter. Beat until the mixture is creamy, then stir in the egg and milk, and mix until smooth. In a small bowl, sift together the flour, salt, and baking powder. Add this to the butter mixture, and beat until smooth. Pour the batter into the prepared pan and spread evenly. Top the batter with the sliced rhubarb, and sprinkle with the gelatin.

Make the topping: Combine the sugar, flour, oats, and butter in a small bowl. Cut with a pastry blender until crumbly. Sprinkle the topping mixture over the batter, and bake for 35 to 40 minutes, until the top is golden brown. Serve warm or cool. Top with whipped cream, if desired.

FROSTED RHUBARB COOKIES
Makes 4 dozen cookies

This is a soft cookie with a subtle rhubarb flavor. It goes great with a cup of coffee or as breakfast. Rhubarb is commonly used in cakes and pies in Amish settlements across the United States, but rhubarb cookies are less common, highlighting Fredonia's rhubarb culinary culture.

1 cup (2 sticks) butter or shortening, softened

1½ cups firmly packed light brown sugar

2 large eggs, beaten

3 cups all-purpose flour

1 teaspoon baking soda

½ teaspoon salt

¾ cup flaked sweetened coconut

1½ cups diced rhubarb

FROSTING

3 ounces cream cheese, softened

1 tablespoon butter, softened

1 tablespoon vanilla extract

1½ cups powdered sugar

Preheat the oven to 350°F.

In a medium mixing bowl, cream the butter and brown sugar until smooth. Add the eggs, one at a time, stirring until well combined. In another, large bowl, sift together the flour, baking soda, and salt. Add this mixture to the batter, and beat until smooth. Fold in the coconut and rhubarb until the ingredients are evenly combined.

Drop the batter by tablespoons onto an ungreased baking sheet. Bake until lightly browned, 12 to 13 minutes. Using a spatula, remove the cookies one by one from the cookie sheet and place on a wire rack to cool completely.

Make the frosting: In a small bowl, beat together the cream cheese, butter, and vanilla until smooth. Gradually add the powdered sugar until the frosting has the consistency that you prefer. Frost the cookies.

RHUBARB TAPIOCA

Makes 4 quarts

Rhubarb adds a festive flair to this normally white-colored dessert. Some people prefer to eat this warm. It also makes a great topping for the Rhubarb Streusel Cake (page 28). If you do not want to make such a large quantity, the recipe can easily be halved. Do not leave this mixture unattended or it will scorch.

1⅓ pounds rhubarb, cut into ½-inch pieces (about 5 cups)
2½ cups water
1¼ cups sugar
¼ cup granulated tapioca

Put the rhubarb and the water in a large stockpot and bring to a boil over medium-high heat. Make sure that it does not boil over, and stir the rhubarb occasionally so it will not scorch. Remove the rhubarb from the heat, stir in the sugar, and very gradually add the tapioca, stirring constantly to avoid clumping. Return the mixture to medium heat and cook until the tapioca is clear, approximately 30 seconds. Remove the mixture from the heat, let it cool, then refrigerate in a sealed container.

FRENCH RHUBARB PIE

Makes one 9-inch pie

Miriam Miller said that French rhubarb pie seems to be a local favorite, especially because so much rhubarb is raised and sold in the community. This pie is a favorite that the Millers sell at a local farmers' market.

1 large egg

1 cup sugar

1 teaspoon vanilla extract

2 tablespoons all-purpose flour

2 cups diced rhubarb

1 (9-inch) unbaked pie shell (see Never-Fail Pastry, page 24)

TOPPING

¾ cup all-purpose flour

½ cup firmly packed brown sugar

5⅓ tablespoons butter

Preheat the oven to 400°F.

Combine the egg, sugar, vanilla, and flour in a large mixing bowl. Stir the mixture until smooth, then fold in the rhubarb. Pour the rhubarb mixture into the pie shell.

Make the topping: Mix the flour and sugar in a bowl. Cut in the butter with a pastry blender to form crumbs. Sprinkle the topping over the rhubarb mixture. Bake the pie for 10 minutes, then decrease the oven temperature to 350°F, and bake until the center is set and the topping is browned, about 30 minutes.

HOMEMADE BAKING MIX

Makes 13 cups

This homemade mix of Miriam Miller's has a variety of uses and saves many trips to the store. The mix is used in cookies, biscuits, cakes, gingerbread, and other baking treats; following the recipe are some of Miriam's suggested uses, provided in her own words.

9 cups sifted all-purpose flour

⅓ cup baking powder

1 tablespoon salt

2 teaspoons cream of tartar

¼ cup sugar

1 cup nonfat dry milk

2 cups shortening

Sift together the sifted flour, baking powder, salt, cream of tartar, sugar, and dry milk. Cut in the shortening until the mixture resembles coarse cornmeal. Store in an airtight container and use as you would use a premeasured baking mix, such as Bisquick (see suggestions on page 33). Place the mix lightly in the desired measuring cup; do not pack it.

MIRIAM MILLER'S
SUGGESTED BAKING MIX USES

These are shorthand suggestions from Miriam Miller as to how her homemade baking mix, on page 32, should be used. These are just guidelines; we recommend comparing your own favorite recipes to these and using the homemade mix where applicable.

Biscuits (1 dozen): 3 cups Homemade Baking Mix, ¾ cup water. Blend only until moistened. Bake at 450°F for 8 to 10 minutes.

Pancakes/waffles (18 medium or 6 large): 3 cups Homemade Baking Mix, 1 egg, 1½ cups water. Blend completely.

Muffins (1 dozen): 3 cups Homemade Baking Mix, 2 tablespoons vegetable oil, 1 egg, 1 cup water. Mix water and egg, blend with dry ingredients, bake at 450°F for 25 minutes.

Gingerbread: 2 cups Homemade Baking Mix, ¼ cup water, 1 egg, ½ cup water, ½ cup molasses, ½ teaspoon ground cinnamon, ½ teaspoon ginger, and ½ teaspoon ground cloves. Beat egg, water, and molasses. Blend dry ingredients. Gradually add liquid. Bake in 8 by 8-inch pan at 350°F for 40 minutes.

Drop cookies: 3 cups Homemade Baking Mix, 1 cup sugar, 1 egg, ⅓ cup water, 1 teaspoon vanilla extract, ½ cup nuts, and ½ cup chocolate chips. Blend and drop mixture on cookie sheet. Bake at 375°F for 10 to 12 minutes.

Coffeecake: 3 cups Homemade Baking Mix, ½ cup sugar, 1 egg, ⅔ cup water. Topping: ½ cup brown sugar, 3 tablespoons butter, ½ teaspoon ground cinnamon, ¼ cup chopped walnuts. Blend. Cover with topping and bake at 400°F for 25 minutes.

Yellow cake or chocolate cake: Use two 8-inch cake pans. 3 cups Homemade Baking Mix, ½ cup sugar, 2 eggs, 1 cup water, 1 teaspoon vanilla extract (½ cup cocoa for chocolate cake). Blend sugar and vanilla into mix. If making a chocolate cake, add the cocoa here. Beat eggs and water. Add additional ½ cup water to the mixture. Beat for 2 minutes and bake at 325°F for 25 minutes.

WHEAT BREAD
Makes 4 loaves

This is one of Miriam Miller's recipes, and she likes to make it in this large quantity so she can freeze the unused portion and have it again later on. She said that the bread never fails to be nice and soft, and that it freezes really well. It's great with butter and rhubarb preserves.

4½ cups water
½ cup coarsely ground wheat flour
¾ cup vegetable oil
1 cup sugar
1 tablespoon salt
2 tablespoons active dry yeast
12 to 13 cups all-purpose flour

Combine 3 cups of the water and the wheat flour in a large pot. Bring to a boil, then cover the pot and remove from the heat. Set aside.

Place the remaining 1½ cups water, the oil, sugar, salt, and yeast in a very large bowl. Stir in the cooled wheat mixture, then add enough of the all-purpose flour to knead into a moderately stiff dough. Let the dough rise until doubled in size, about 30 minutes.

Punch down the dough, then shape it into four loaves. Let the loaves rise until they are doubled in size, about 30 minutes.

Preheat the oven to 325°F. When the dough has risen, bake the loaves until they are nicely browned, about 40 minutes.

DOVER, DELAWARE

AT A GLANCE

Date established: 1915

Number of church districts: 10

Culinary highlights: seafood

Dover, Delaware, enjoys a distinction not found among any other state capital in the United States.

"It's the only capital where you can see buggies in the streets," chuckled an Amish woman who once lived in the Dover settlement.

And there's this very stark distinction about the Delaware Amish:

"People might not realize that the State of Delaware only allows the Amish to settle in three counties," explained Dorothy Byler, an Amish woman who lives in the Dover settlement. Of course, Delaware only has three counties," she continued, with deadpan punch-line accuracy. Dorothy Byler is a scribe for the *Budget* (see page 127) describing the comings, goings, and happenings in her settlement.

Ten Amish parochial schools are spread out among the ten different districts, so no scholar, as the Amish refer to their students, ever has to walk very far. The church districts are clustered west of the city of Dover out in the countryside, where plenty of Amish home-based businesses from greenhouses to bakeries to bulk food stores dot the rural roads.

One of the highlights of this low-key community is an annual bike tour that attracts many out-of-state visitors to what is billed as the "Amish Country Bike Tour." There are five different distances that participants can pedal: 15, 25, 50, 62, and 100 miles. This

variety attracts anyone from the casual cyclists to the Tour de France wannabes. The event is a tour, not a race. Participants just come to bike and enjoy the scenery. The irony is that the Dover Amish communities—like many settlements elsewhere—don't permit bikes.

As Cindy Small, Dover resident and executive director of Kent County & Greater Dover, Delaware Convention and Visitors Bureau, described the terrain, "It's flat; you could try to roll a quarter and it wouldn't go anyplace."

The bike tour's name is more than just window dressing; the Amish really do involve themselves in the festivities.

"The very first scene our cyclists see is an Amish gentleman by the name of Ben Miller who brings his horse and buggy into town and leads the cyclists through the historic town of Dover all the way to the city line, and he then pulls away and the cyclists are off. You look and it is a huge number of cyclists coming down the road with an Amish buggy in front of them," Small noted. Some years, up to 1,800 cyclists participate.

The first stop on the tour is at one of the Amish schoolhouses, which is billed as a "pie stop." Byler's Bakery (not directly related to Dorothy Byler) bakes up to two hundred blueberry, cherry, pumpkin, and apple pies for the cyclists. The rest of the routes then meander through the flat, picturesque Amish country.

Some Amish children excitedly anticipate the passing cyclists and they'll sit on split-rail fences in their straw hats and suspenders, waving to participants. And at the end of the tour: Amish ice cream.

"An Amish man makes homemade ice cream and comes to the headquarters, so when people get finished with the ride, he is there with homemade ice cream for sale. A John Deere machine makes the ice cream—never seen anything like it. He tows it into town behind the horse and buggy, gets the motor running, and somehow this contraption makes homemade ice cream," Small said.

Here is a recipe from the Delaware Amish:

SHRIMP SALAD SANDWICHES
Makes 8 sandwiches

Fresh shrimp are plentiful in the temperate Atlantic waters off Delaware. This is a refreshing way to enjoy these delicacies on a warm summer day.

8 ounces cream cheese, softened
¼ cup sour cream
½ teaspoon dried dill
⅛ teaspoon salt
8 ounces fresh shrimp, cooked, shells removed
½ cup chopped green bell pepper
⅓ cup chopped onion
1 cup chopped tomato
1 (8-roll) tube crescent rolls
½ cup cocktail sauce
½ cup shredded Monterey Jack cheese

Cream together the cream cheese, sour cream, dill, and salt in a medium mixing bowl. Chop the cooked shrimp, and stir into the cream cheese mixture until well combined. Refrigerate until chilled, about 1 hour.

Mix the chopped vegetables together in a bowl.

Bake the crescent rolls according to the package directions. Split the baked rolls lengthwise and spread a portion of the shrimp salad inside each roll. Top each with 1 tablespoon of the cocktail sauce, a portion of the chopped vegetables, and a portion of the cheese.

AMISH COOK SPECIAL RECIPE
BY LOVINA EICHER

FISH LOAF
Serves 4 to 6

Fishing is a favorite pastime among Amish here in Michigan and elsewhere. My husband, Joe, likes to go fishing, and even does ice fishing on occasion when it is cold enough and he has the time.

1 pound fresh fish (bluegill, bass) diced,
   or 1 (15-ounce) can salmon (see Note)
2 large eggs
1 teaspoon dry mustard
¾ teaspoon salt

⅛ teaspoon black pepper ½ cup milk
½ cup chopped celery
2 cups dried bread crumbs
3 tablespoons finely chopped fresh parsley
2 tablespoons minced onion

Preheat the oven to 375°F.

    If using canned fish, do not drain. If using fresh fish, remove the skin and bones. Place the diced fish in a large mixing bowl.

    In a separate small bowl, beat the eggs with the mustard, salt, and pepper. Mix in the milk, celery, bread crumbs, parsley, and onion with a fork. Add the egg mixture to the fish and stir to combine. Pack the mixture into a greased 9 by 12-inch or smaller pan. Bake for 45 minutes, or until the top begins to turn golden brown. Slice and serve warm.

Note from Kevin: Fish catches vary from settlement to settlement. In Amish settlements out west, salmon is a favorite freshwater catch; in the cold creeks of Maine, it is trout. In southern Amish communities, catfish is king. This recipe of Lovina's can be used with a variety of freshwater or sea fish, such as those found in the waters of Delaware.

LYNDONVILLE, NEW YORK

AT A GLANCE

Date established: 1998

Number of church districts: 2

Culinary highlights: apples

The Lyndonville area is typical of the rapid growth in Amish population that New York State has been experiencing. The Empire State once had Amish communities primarily in the far southwest of the state (see Conewango Valley, page 2), but the first decade after the year 2000 saw settlements sprout throughout the Finger Lakes, the Mohawk Valley, and even in the North Country, more known for its Adirondack Mountains and proximity to French-speaking Quebec than for its horse-and-buggy culture.

Gracia Schlabach's story is similar to that of many other recent Amish arrivals to New York State.

"There was a real estate ad . . . where we first heard that there were farms available in this area. There were a lot of older farmers retiring and farmland coming up for sale," she recalled.

Gracia Schlabach is a resident of the Lyndonville Amish community, which is only about 3 miles from the southern shore of Lake Ontario. New York has seen about a dozen new Amish settlements establish themselves in the first years of the twenty-first century. Almost all of the Amish in the small settlement in Lyndonville have their roots in Holmes County, Ohio. In New York, they found the space that Ohio was lacking. The Young Center for Anabaptist Studies at Elizabethtown College in Pennsylvania cited New York State in 2010 for having the fastest-growing Amish population of any state. Many small-town, Upstate New York residents have welcomed the Amish, who have economically invigorated the area with their small businesses and entrepreneurial spirit.

"Overall we received a very warm welcome. People were glad to see abandoned farmsteads cleaned up and made productive again. We received a very good welcome," Schlabach said. "There were people wanting to do more agricultural livelihoods. And another reason to come was simply to expand the church planting efforts."

This is an area known for its plentiful apple orchards. Popular apple varieties grown here include Golden Delicious, McIntosh, Ginger Gold, Jonagold, Gala, and Empire. The Empire is New York's State Apple and a hybrid of the Red Delicious and McIntosh variety. The Jonagold apple is a popular apple developed by non-Amish farmers in the Lyndonville area. But the Amish are in on the apple action. Gracia Schlabach's family runs Schlabach's Nursery, which ships out more than fifty varieties of heirloom apple trees all over the country.

"Apples are our specialty," she said of the nursery, which her family established in Ohio in 1991. "After we came here, we had more land. Our nursery fits in nicely because we get to interact with people developing new varieties of apples. We also do test-growing for Cornell University, which complements our pursuits nicely."

Apples are such a staple of this settlement, according to Schlabach, that they are an important baking ingredient in pies, cakes, bars, and dumplings. Frequently, sliced fresh apples are on the menu at mealtime. Some families also dry apples. "And what is better than spicy apple butter on freshly baked bread?" she said. Apples are so popular here that sometimes fresh apple butter is served instead of the traditional peanut butter spread after church services.

Apples are also used frequently to make homemade applesauce, apple pie filling, and apple dumplings. Schlabach said that many Amish cooks in the community like to halve and core apples, add some spices, put a dough around the apples, then freeze them. When they want fresh apple dumplings, all they do is thaw and bake them. The Amish of Lyndonville also freeze and can a lot of the homemade cider they hand-press in the fall. "Gala apples press out really nicely," she said.

Apples are also featured prominently in the important potlucks and after-church meals. "We frequently have apple slices to pass around at church. Sometimes when we have carry-in lunches, we'll have a platter full of apple slices and a big toteful of apple slices for everyone to enjoy."

And how about the problem of keeping sliced apples from turning an unappetizing brown after sitting out and being passed around?

"Certain kinds of apples brown easily," Schlabach said. "So part of it depends on what kind you use, but if appearance is important, then dip the apples in a solution of a few drops of lemon in water." The citric acid will keep them from getting brown.

Schlabach likes to peel her apples with a cranked apple peeler and then use a corer that works by pressing down on the top.

"Those are nice. We use those a lot."

And she described her favorite way to fix apples as a snack.

"Any meal or coffee break is enhanced with a large plate of slices of apples, oranges, bananas, kiwi, raw pineapple, and grapes (as the center). There is more awareness of sugarless eating, and any host should make this possible for the guests who are invited. The more you do to an apple, the less healthy it may become."

TRUSTY APPLE DESSERT

Serves 12 to 14

Gracia Schlabach said this dessert is delicious served with ice cream. Or she lets it cool before topping it with a creamy topping. This is a good eggless dessert to serve. And if you like crunch, she said, add walnut pieces.

2 medium-size apples
  (Red Delicious or Gala),
  peeled and shredded

1 cup sugar

2 tablespoons butter, softened

2 cups all-purpose flour

1 cup milk

2 rounded teaspoons
  baking powder

1 tablespoon ground cinnamon

1 teaspoon vanilla extract

Pinch of salt

SYRUP

1½ cups firmly packed
  brown sugar

1½ cups water

2 tablespoons butter, melted

1 tablespoon imitation
  maple flavoring

Preheat the oven to 350°F.

Place the shredded apples in the bottom of a 9 by 9-inch baking pan. Combine the sugar, butter, flour, milk, baking powder, cinnamon, vanilla, and salt in a large bowl. Mix until smooth and well combined. Pour the dough mixture on top of the grated apples.

Make the syrup: In another bowl, combine the brown sugar, water, butter, and maple flavoring. Pour the syrup mixture over the top of the dough. Bake for 35 to 40 minutes, until bubbly and the center is set.

SOUR CREAM APPLE PIE

Makes one 9-inch pie

This is a delicious apple pie with a hint of crunch on the crust from its crumb topping. The crumb topping recipe can easily be doubled or tripled for use on additional pies.

8 to 10 medium-size apples
  (such as Ida Red or Golden
  Delicious), peeled and sliced

1 (9-inch) unbaked pie shell

4 large eggs, beaten

1½ cups sugar

¼ cup all-purpose flour

2 teaspoons vanilla extract

2 teaspoons ground cinnamon

½ teaspoon salt

2 cups sour cream

CRUMB TOPPING

¾ cup all-purpose flour

½ cup firmly packed
  brown sugar

⅓ cup butter, softened

Preheat the oven to 325°F.

Place the apple slices in the pie shell. Mix the eggs, sugar, flour, vanilla, cinnamon, salt, and sour cream in a large mixing bowl. Pour the mixture into the pie shell over the apple slices.

Make the crumb topping: In a small mixing bowl, mix the flour, brown sugar, and softened butter, using your fingers, until the mixture resembles coarse crumbs. Top the apple mixture with a generous layer of the crumbs. Bake for 35 to 40 minutes, until the pie is solid when jiggled.

AMISH COOK SPECIAL RECIPE
BY LOVINA EICHER

APPLE BREAD

Makes 1 large loaf

Like the Lyndonville Amish, we make a lot of apple bread and apple butter. We bake a lot of apple bread in the community. This bread goes fast around here when it is baked. I usually use Jonathan apples, which are plentiful in Michigan.

½ cup (1 stick) butter or shortening, softened

1¼ cups sugar

2 large eggs

2 teaspoons baking powder

½ teaspoon ground cinnamon

2 cups all-purpose flour

1 teaspoon salt

¼ teaspoon ground nutmeg

1½ cups finely grated apples

Preheat the oven to 350°F.

Cream together the butter and sugar in a large mixing bowl. Add the eggs, one at a time, beating well after each addition. In a separate bowl, sift together the baking powder, cinnamon, flour, salt, and nutmeg. Add the sifted ingredients to the creamed mixture, and stir until well combined. Fold in the grated apples. Pour the batter into a greased 5 by 9-inch loaf pan, and bake for 1 hour, or until golden.

SNITZ HALF-MOON PIES
Makes about 12 small pies

Snitz *apples are a staple among the Amish.* Snitz *simply means "dried." Homemade dried apples can be made in several ways; many Amish cooks use their ovens at a low setting for an all-day drying of the apples.*

3 cups water

2 quarts dried apple slices (apple *snitz*),
 preferably Cortland or Empire variety

1½ cups firmly packed brown sugar

½ teaspoon salt

½ teaspoon ground cinnamon

Pie dough for 2 (9-inch) double-crust pies
 (see Never-Fail Pastry, page 24)

Place the water and apple slices in a 4-quart pot. Cover and simmer for 20 to 30 minutes, until the apples are soft and look like the apple slices in a traditional apple pie. Add water to the pot if the water boils off and the apples are not yet soft enough.

Remove the apples from the heat. Strain and return to the pot. Add the brown sugar, salt, and cinnamon, and mix well with the apples.

Preheat the oven to 450°F. Roll out each portion of pie dough, and cut out twelve 7- to 8-inch circles. Using a fork, pierce one-half of each circle with a couple of small holes to allow steam to vent. Place ½ cup of the filling on the other half of each circle. Wet the circles' edges, fold over the dough so that the filling is on one side of the crease, and smooth the dough over the filling so that air pockets will not form inside the pie. Press the edges together and seal them firmly all the way around the half-moon. Be sure there are no gaps, to prevent filling from escaping.

Bake the half-moon pies on ungreased baking sheets for 15 to 20 minutes, or until the edges of the crust are golden brown and the tops of the pies are beginning to brown.

APPLE FRY PIES
Makes about 40 pies

Fry pies are an Amish tradition and a staple in the kitchen of most Amish bakers. Filled with fresh apples and drizzled with a hot, sugary glaze, they become an amazing snack. These pies are often sold for fund-raisers. An Amish settlement might have a "fry pie" drive to raise money for a church member's medical bills. These are also snacks made and sold where there are large public gatherings such as an auction or sale, which is why this recipe is often made in such large batches. Store any leftovers uncovered to prevent the pies from getting soggy.

9 cups cake flour

1 teaspoon salt

2 tablespoons sugar

3 cups shortening

2 cups water

2½ cups of your favorite apple pie filling

Vegetable oil, for deep-frying

GLAZE

4 pounds powdered sugar

¼ cup cornstarch

¼ cup evaporated milk

½ teaspoon vanilla extract

1¼ cups water

Combine the cake flour, salt, and sugar in a large bowl. Cut in the shortening to form coarse crumbs. Add the water and mix to form a pie dough. Roll out the dough and cut out forty 7- or 8-inch circles. Moisten the edges of the dough with water. Place 1 tablespoon of the apple pie filling on half of each circle. Fold over the dough and smooth the dough over the filling so that air pockets will not form inside the pie. Press the edges together and seal them firmly all the way around the half-moon. Be sure there are no gaps to prevent filling from escaping. Crimp the edges with a fork.

Fill a large kettle half full with vegetable oil and heat the oil to a temperature of 350°F. Deep-fry the pies until golden brown, about 1 minute on each side. Use tongs or a slotted spoon to turn over the fried pies. Be careful of splattering oil. Drain and let cool completely on wire racks set over paper towels.

Make the glaze: In a large mixing bowl, combine the powdered sugar, cornstarch, evaporated milk, vanilla, and water. Stir until well mixed and smooth. When the pies have cooled, dip them in the glaze and place on wire racks set over paper towels to catch the excess that drips off.

AMISH COOKS ACROSS THE
MIDWEST

After the Amish had settled in Pennsylvania and Delaware in sufficient numbers, they began exploring new horizons to the west, an exploration that continues to this day. Ohio and Indiana were the states with the largest early concentrations of Amish, but now Illinois, Missouri, Kansas, Iowa, Michigan, Wisconsin, and Minnesota enjoy large Amish populations. The Dakotas were largely claimed by the Hutterites, but recently some Amish have begun to discover the area. South Dakota had its first Amish settlement established near the town of Tripp in 2011.

The Midwest Amish have a lot of culinary and cultural variety—a surprising amount. The postcard hills of Holmes County, Ohio, are teeming with Amish and tourists. But Ohio also has other sizable settlements, from Geauga County's sprawling Amish community about 50 miles east of Cleveland to the flinty, hardscrabble hills of Adams County, home to another large settlement on the edge of Appalachia.

In Indiana, the Amish in the northern part of the state tie their fortunes to the rise or fall of the ubiquitous RV factories. The Amish around Berne retain their own distinctive Swiss settlement (see page 88) and more conservative, quieter communities dot the southern part of the state. Pennsylvania Amish have moved relatively recently to Parke County and Wayne County, Indiana, bringing with them their Lancaster customs.

Amish growth in Illinois has been relatively slow over the years. The state's largest and oldest Old Order community continues to be around the Arthur-Arcola area, with its distinctive "shop culture" of small businesses and home enterprises.

Missouri is home to the nation's other large settlement of Swiss Amish, located just outside Seymour in the far southwest, while other more traditional communities of Amish can be found around Bowling Green and Jamesport. Neighboring Iowa has also had a steady Amish presence, especially in the eastern half of the state.

Nebraska (not to be confused with the Nebraska Amish; see page 1) has a scant Amish population, with a single community located near Orchard. And in Kansas, the Amish's oldest settlement can be found around the town of Yoder, but other communities are now scattered throughout the state.

Wisconsin has seen its Amish population surge in recent years. Amish settlements can be found in all parts of the state, but the biggest boom has occurred around the town of Cashton in the rural west. And the Amish have increasingly been drawn to Minnesota. The state's largest settlement can be found in the relatively "warm" southeast part of the state near Harmony, although communities can now be found throughout the state.

We'll start our visit with Amish cooks across the Midwest in a very conservative settlement in sparsely populated southern Ohio.

SINKING SPRING, OHIO

AT A GLANCE

Date established: 2006

Number of church districts: 1

Culinary highlights: traditional Amish

Massive, boulder-crushing glaciers pressed most of Ohio flapjack flat, but the ice sheets couldn't conquer the southeast part of the state. So on a seam where central Ohio's farm fields meet the foothills of Appalachia, a community of self-sufficient Swartzentrubers has taken root, living off the land and scratching out a living from whatever's available.

Gender roles in Old Order society are very well defined in almost every church but perhaps nowhere more so than among the Swartzentruber Amish.

The men have made the rocky fields of deep east Highland County arable, growing oats, corn, hay, and spelt, while the women tend to the home fires, crafting homemade cheeses, cereals, and soaps. The closest town is a speck of a settlement, the village of Sinking Spring, named for a small subterranean flow outside town. Sinking Spring has welcomed its new ultraconservative Amish neighbors, erecting hitching posts outside of some businesses in town and just generally leaving the Swartzentrubers alone, which is the way they like it.

"From my experiences they have been accepted by the locals with no problems. The only real problem was with teaching locals to be more aware and careful of more horse and buggies on the roads," said Brad Bergeford, horticultural specialist with the Ohio State University Extension Office.

Considered a subgroup of the Old Order Amish that split off in the early twentieth century, the Swartzentrubers, named after one of the first bishops of the sect, are among the most conservative of Amish groups. Like most Amish, they shun electricity and cars, but they also eschew indoor plumbing, buttons, and bicycles. Clothing is fastened with straight pins. Interaction with outsiders is discouraged. Swartzentruber buggies don't display the orange slow-moving-vehicle safety triangle usually used to alert motorists. Instead, they use gray reflective tape on the back borders of their buggies—or nothing at all. Motorists visiting the area need to be extra alert after dark, when black buggies can blend seamlessly into a velvet night.

The Swartzentruber sect was once primarily found in Wayne and Holmes counties, Ohio, and that is still where the largest concentration resides. But now groups of Swartzentrubers can be found in fifteen states.

Twenty families of Swartzentruber Amish call the area along Sinking Spring Road home. The first groups moved to the sparsely populated area from increasingly crowded Wayne County in 2006. "You can turn around here," one Amish man said, referring to the clogged roads, tourist buses, and high land prices found in areas to the north.

Basket making has become a popular pastime among the Sinking Spring Swartzentrubers. Eli and Mattie Stutzman and

their eight children weave handmade baskets from a shop on their property. More than eighty varieties of woven wonders, from elaborate cedar clothes hampers to simple bread baskets, adorn their store. The items are inscribed with the name of the person who made it. A small bread basket has "Ammon, age 12," written on it. The Stutzmans also farm and sell produce from a rambling garden. Mattie Stutzman puts a few jars of homemade relish or jellies to sell in their basket shop. The Zook family down the road does the same. The steep limestone hills that mark the edge of the glacial advance tower to the north and east. The oldest Stutzman daughter, Amanda, works part-time during the spring at a nearby greenhouse, tending to and nurturing plants.

A chorus of purple martins sing chaotically outside the Stutzman home. "One of my wishes came true; I had always wanted these," Eli Stutzman said, surveying the three towering purple martin houses that he made himself. Each of his bird-size "apartments" has fourteen units.

On a warm spring afternoon, the Stutzmans sat on their porch, watching the purple martins play and hearing the spring breezes swirl through their garden. The Swartzentruber Amish may have a reputation for being stern and unwelcoming, but the Stutzmans were completely the opposite. The inside of their home was a tidy, old-fashioned tableau of nineteenth-century simplicity.

Mattie Stutzman makes meals on a wood-burning stove in a tidy kitchen with powder blue walls and shiny cabinets. The kitchen is infused with the smells of toasted grains, fresh vegetables, and freshly baked bread.

The Stutzmans grow and mill their own oats, which they bake into cookies, blend into homemade cereals, and shape into tasty "energy bars" cut into thick squares.

"Try one," Mattie Stutzman offers. And I happily oblige, finding the bars a delicious combination of crunchy and chewy.

"We try to make as much of our own as possible," she said, which would also include cereal, yogurt, cheese, and other staples.

HOMEMADE CEREAL
Makes about 24 cups

Even the most conservative Amish will go to a bulk food store to stock up on tasty treats they can't really make, such as marshmallows, graham crackers, and some store-bought cereals. This is a favorite recipe for what the Stutzmans declare to be a "delicious breakfast cereal." The family stores the cereal in large sealable containers, which keep it dry and fresh so it can be enjoyed for weeks. This recipe can be halved for a more manageable amount.

14 cups quick-cooking oats

1 cup honey

1¼ cups vegetable oil

4 cups crisped-rice cereal, such as Rice Krispies

1 pound shredded sweetened coconut

1 sleeve graham crackers (8 to 10 crackers), crumbled but not crushed

1½ teaspoons salt

1 tablespoon vanilla extract

Preheat the oven to 350°F.

Combine all the ingredients in a large bowl or stockpot until well blended. Spread in a thin layer on five baking sheets and bake until the coconut begins to turn golden brown, 20 to 25 minutes, stirring occasionally.

DELICIOUS APPLE CAKE
Serves 14 to 16

This cake can be served immediately or after cooling, and it's good plain or with vanilla ice cream.

2 large eggs, beaten

1½ cups vegetable oil

3 cups all-purpose flour

2 cups sugar

½ teaspoon salt

1 teaspoon baking soda

1½ teaspoons ground cinnamon

3 cups diced apples (see Note)

½ cup raisins (optional)

Preheat the oven to 350°F. Grease and flour a 9 by 13-inch pan and set aside.

Mix together the eggs, oil, flour, sugar, salt, baking soda, and cinnamon in a large bowl until well blended. Add the apples and raisins. The batter will be doughlike, and it may be necessary to knead in the apples and raisins to fully incorporate them. Spread the batter evenly into the prepared pan. Bake for 1 hour, or until the top is golden brown and the edges are firm.

Note: Any variety of apple will work fine, but slightly tart apples will lend more flavor to the cake.

HOMEMADE GRANOLA BARS
Makes 28 to 32 bars

Tiring days spent outside in the sun-baked fields far from the house can call for a portable snack. Long before grocery stores starting selling prepackaged, processed granola bars, the Amish were making their own—like these.

5 cups quick-cooking oats

4½ cups crisped-rice cereal, such as Rice Krispies

2 cups chocolate chips

1 sleeve graham crackers (8 to 10 crackers), crushed

12 tablespoons unsalted butter

¼ cup peanut butter

¼ cup vegetable oil

¼ cup honey

2 (10-ounce) packages mini marshmallows

Lightly grease a 10 by 15-inch pan and set aside.

Combine the oats, rice cereal, chocolate chips, and graham cracker crumbs in a large bowl and stir until well blended. Set aside. Melt the butter, peanut butter, oil, honey, and marshmallows in a large saucepan. Stir well until the mixture is evenly melted and smooth, then add to the dry ingredients and mix until thoroughly combined. Spread the mixture into the prepared pan, let cool, then cut into bars.

BAKED CHOCOLATE FUDGE PUDDING
Serves 14 to 16

The Swartzentruber Amish are known for their from-scratch simplicity. And even the most conservative groups get the urge for a sweet treat. This dessert is often the answer.

3 tablespoons shortening

¾ cup granulated sugar

1 cup all-purpose flour

1½ teaspoons baking powder

¾ teaspoon salt

½ cup milk

1 cup firmly packed brown sugar

¼ cup unsweetened cocoa powder

1¼ cups boiling water

Preheat the oven to 350°F.

Cream together the shortening and granulated sugar in a large mixing bowl. In a small bowl, combine the flour, baking powder, and ½ teaspoon of the salt. Add this mixture, alternately with the milk, to the creamed mixture. Pour into an ungreased 8 by 8-inch pan.

Mix the brown sugar, cocoa powder, and the remaining ¼ teaspoon salt in a small bowl, sprinkle the mixture over the batter, then pour the boiling water over the batter. Bake until the pudding is set, 45 to 50 minutes.

MAKING LYE SOAP

Mattie Stutzman enjoys makes her own soap, citing the lack of chemicals in it and the fact that it saves money and trips into town. Her soap forms solid, fragrant blocks that last longer than most store-bought bars and leave a refreshing feel after washing. It's a complex process, requiring precision and up to several days, but one batch will produce thirty-two 2-inch bars of soap. The process ends with the soap mixture's cooling (which could take a full day), and curing (which could take as long as 3 weeks). If you want to try it yourself at home, please read the cautions and recipe carefully first.

CAUTIONS

- Lye is caustic until it is cured and its fumes should not be inhaled. Protective gloves and safety goggles should be worn when working with lye or lye solutions, as chemical burns can occur on the skin, mucous membranes, and even the throat and lungs. The work area must be very well ventilated. Lye soap should be made outside, but if it is to be made inside, a fan and an open window are highly desirable.

- Vinegar should be kept handy during lye soap making to neutralize any splashes or spills of lye, lye water, or uncured soap, which are extremely alkaline.

- No copper, tin, or aluminum materials can be used for this process, as a dangerous chemical reaction can occur. Materials used to make lye soap should only be used for making soap and should never be reused for food preparation or other uses. Items should be clearly marked for soap making only and kept stored safely when not in use. Anything the lye or lye water or uncured soap touches is then caustic.

- Ingredients should be measured carefully, as mistakes can cause the saponification process to fail and the soap may be unusable.

INGREDIENTS

1 quart water

12 ounces lye (100% sodium hydroxide),
    containing no dark spots, which are undesirable heavy metals

2½ quarts clean lard or tallow, melted

MATERIALS

2-quart or larger crock, Pyrex measuring cup (must be Pyrex, as nontempered glass
    will break), or heavy plastic pitcher

Wooden stirring spoon, or heat-resistant rubber or silicone spatula

Container, to hold stirring utensils that have touched lye

2 candy thermometers

12-quart clean dishpan or other plastic storage container. Clear works best so you can see
    if there are spots where the lye has failed to combine properly with the fat.

Essential oil or soap-making scent, if desired

Lid for the container (does not have to be tightly fitting)

Towels or blanket, to keep the soap warm for a few days

Knife, to cut the soap after it has set up, before it has cured

White freezer paper, white plastic mesh, or another clean white surface

Put the water in the crock. Add the lye and stir gently, being careful not to cause any splashes, until the lye is dissolved. IMPORTANT: The lye must be poured into the water, and never the other way around.

Let the lye water stand until lukewarm, 90° to 95°F. Let the melted fat stand until lukewarm or no more than 100°F. These temperatures must be reached simultaneously. If the fat is not cooling quickly enough, it can be placed in a sink of cold or iced water. If the fat cools too much before the lye water is ready, it can be rewarmed on the stove. Once both substances are the correct temperature, pour the fat in the large dishpan. Pour the lye water slowly into the fat while stirring, and continue stirring constantly for 15 minutes to 1 hour. When the soap is ready to set up, it will "trace": The track of the spoon will stay evident in the mixture. At this point, a few drops of essential oil or soap fragrance can be stirred in, if desired.

Once the soap traces, the container should be covered and wrapped in a towel, blanket, or even old pillow cases to slow the cooling process so the soap won't separate. The container should not be disturbed for at least 24 hours. The soap can be checked about every half hour after the stirring has stopped, to see whether it is ready to be cut. To be cut, the soap should have attained a firm, butterlike consistency. A sharp knife should be used to cut the soap into bars. The soap is still caustic at this time, so avoid contact with your skin.

All equipment should be washed immediately. Be sure to wear gloves. The containers should be rinsed well in warm water to remove all traces of soap, lye, and fat, and then washed in warm, soapy water.

After 24 hours, look through the sides of the container. All surfaces of the soap should appear solid. The bars should be hard and easily removed from the plastic container, but in some cases this process may take up to 3 days. Many factors affect the length of time the soap takes to harden. The bars are ready to be turned out of the container when they do not accept finger indentations (use gloves to test). In a cool place on white freezer paper, stack or space the bars with open spaces in between, to allow good airflow. The bars should be allowed 2 to 3 weeks to cure before use. The longer the curing period, the harder the soap. If the soap is allowed to cure for 3 to 4 weeks, the bars are safe to be wrapped in paper, if desired.

FLAT ROCK, ILLINOIS

AT A GLANCE
Date established: 1995
Number of church districts: 1
Culinary highlights: venison

Tucked away along a grid of gravel roads in far southeast Illinois, Flat Rock is in "no-man's-land," at least an hour by car from anywhere. It has to be one of the most unusual Amish enclaves in the country. With the largest and oldest Amish settlement in Illinois just 100 miles away, a visitor could easily be taken aback by how out of the way Flat Rock is. Maps and a GPS didn't help much, but a good sense of smell did. If the wind is right, the smell of chocolate lingers in the air from the Hershey factory in the nearby town of Robinson. A prison and a refinery also keep this small city busier than its size would seem.

Flat Rock is about 15 miles south of Robinson. The drive in a buggy from Flat Rock to the Walmart in Robinson takes about 45 minutes, so trips into town by horse and buggy are infrequent.

The Amish settlement at Flat Rock is tiny—only about one hundred Amish spread through sixteen families. What the church lacks in size, it makes up for in heart. Without a network of other Amish churches nearby (the closest other Amish settlements are hours away by buggy), the Flat Rock congregants are like one large family. In fact, some might call this settlement the "Flat Rock Family" because the church pulls together as one. And unlike some smaller settlements that are wary of outsiders, Flat Rock Amish are welcoming.

Flat Rock's isolation has shaped its culinary traditions. An Amish-run grocery store supplies most of the store-bought staples. Meat is raised and butchered in Flat Rock, and the ample deer population roaming the hills of southern Illinois are a prime source of food.

"Beef is a real treat for me. I never buy beef because I always have so much venison on hand," said Dorcas Raber, sitting on the porch of her home. The Rabers live on 90 acres, where her husband, David, also owns and operates a wood shop that makes and sells rustic furniture.

"I'd call the cooking style here a little simpler," she said. You won't find some of the more involved recipes used in Amish settlements out east.

The Flat Rock Amish maintain a 15-acre watermelon field that they harvest and sell once a year to raise funds for their school. The church youth also occasionally serve meals to the public in nearby Robinson as school fund-raisers.

"We church ladies all make something for the youth suppers; we all are assigned our portion to make for the supper," Raber said. The meals are usually held about three times a year.

The events are open to the whole community, Amish and non-Amish, and usually offer a meat, mashed potatoes, vegetables, salad, Amish peanut butter spread, homemade bread, ice cream, and pie. Pecan and various fruit pies are usually on the menu.

"Whoever is on the school board is in charge of helping the youth," Raber said. The visitors come in, pay, take their plates, and go past the youth in the serving line, who dish out the mashed

potatoes and other foods. The youth comprise the unmarrieds in the church, anyone fifteen years old and up.

"Whatever we make off the suppers goes to the school fund to pay the teachers," Raber said. Usually most of the Flat Rock church shows up, along with people from Robinson, so about 250 to 300 people come for a typical supper. That means there's a lot of food; about 90 pounds of potatoes are mashed for each of the suppers.

The school suppers and watermelon drives are just a couple of the activities that give Flat Rock a real family feel.

"The church family is what really makes me love it here," Raber said.

Another hallmark of the Flat Rock community are the Bible verses that church members display on plain black-and-white signs at the ends of their driveways. Evangelizing has historically been something the Amish church has avoided, but these signs, while not subtle, are pretty mainstream verses that have broad appeal.

The style of buggies reflects the eclectic mix of plain people found here. There are open buggies, closed buggies, and wagons, and one older couple even retrofitted a golf cart to turn it into a buggy: The Amish man gutted the innards of the cart, added some buggy shafts, and painted it black. The result is a low-riding "buggy" that makes stepping in and out easier than it is in the higher vehicles.

The surrounding fields and hills are teeming with white-tailed deer, which are the prime meat source for Flat Rock residents. When deer season arrives, the men and the boys—and even the girls and

women—take to the thick forests for a chance at some venison. The meat is turned into burgers, steaks, and other such creations.

Summers in downstate Illinois can be as sultry as any in Dixie. In fact, Flat Rock is on the same latitude as northern Kentucky and Richmond, Virginia, so in some ways it feels more Southern than Midwestern. On a July day, with temperatures close to one hundred, Dorcas Raber found a creative solution for beating the heat. She simply moved her whole family—kitchen and everything—to the relative cool of the basement. A couple of her children were sitting comfortably on rockers, reading, as this makeshift kitchen had provided all the essentials.

"We'll move back upstairs when the weather cools down," Raber said.

That type of Amish ingenuity is very endearing. Moving to the cellar is certainly not a groundbreaking act, but the Rabers had moved *everything* to the basement. A lot of non-Amish might have complained about doing that, but the Rabers just seemed to effortlessly and seamlessly resettle. The only trace of family life upstairs was a quilt being pieced together on a table.

Just down the road on adjoining property live one of the Rabers' daughters, Gloria Yoder, and her husband, Daniel, who showed some amazing hospitality and eyes for decor. She had prepared a superb spread of barbecued venison meatballs, green beans, strawberry ice cream, and Flat Rock pudding. The venison meatballs were melt-in-your-mouth amazing and the fresh-from-the-garden green beans equally tasty. The homemade strawberry ice cream was just the antidote for the unforgiving July heat.

"Homemade ice cream melts a lot faster than the store-bought kind, so you might want to eat it kind of quickly," Gloria said, laughing, as she eyed a rapidly liquefying bowl of ice cream.

And her food looked wonderful. Although she was only twenty, Gloria Yoder had the confidence and flair of someone who had been in the food-styling business for years. Gloria and Daniel welcomed their first baby, Julia, into the world in September 2011.

Across the street from the Yoders is the 15-acre watermelon patch. In August, the melons would be at their ripe prime and ready to pick. And so the whole church community would gather on a single day later in the summer and pick all the melons. But this day was simply broiling, so the important thing was that the melons didn't fry right there on the vine.

The Amish settlement in Flat Rock embodies a lot of the characteristics and qualities that people find fascinating and endearing about the Amish. An encounter on the way out of Flat Rock gave a visitor an unforgettable look at these folks. The visitor stopped at a roadside produce stand and bought some fresh tomatoes and cucumbers from an Amish man. They enjoyed some small talk, and the visitor explained why he, a non-Amish outsider, had been poking around. He left his business card as part of his explanation. On the way home, a glance at the math showed that the teenage girl at the stand had overcharged for the produce by a few dollars. Oh, well, she was young, it wasn't much money, and mistakes happen. But a few days later, the mail brought a note from the girl and a check for the difference.

BARBECUED VENISON MEATBALLS
Serves 6 to 8

The barbecue sauce, which carries a hint of tang and a suggestion of sweetness, smothers any "gamey" taste to this local delicacy.

3 pounds ground venison

1¾ cups milk

1 cup quick-cooking oats

1 cup saltine cracker crumbs

3 large eggs, beaten

1 teaspoon chili powder

1 teaspoon onion salt

1 teaspoon garlic salt

Salt and black pepper

BARBECUE SAUCE

2 cups ketchup

¾ cup firmly packed brown sugar

1 tablespoon prepared mustard

1 tablespoon vinegar

1½ teaspoons liquid smoke

Preheat the oven to 350°F.

Place all the meatball ingredients in a large bowl. Stir or knead until the meat mixture is well combined. Shape the meat into 1½-inch balls, place the balls on baking sheets, and bake for 15 to 20 minutes, until the meat is no longer pink inside.

While the meatballs are baking, make the barbecue sauce. Place all the sauce ingredients in a Dutch oven and stir until they are well combined. Cook over medium heat, stirring frequently, until the mixture almost boils. Add the baked meatballs to the sauce, decrease the heat to medium-low, and simmer until ready to serve.

FLAT ROCK PUDDING
Serves 8 to 12

Dorcas Raber said this dessert originated when a woman in her church used chocolate chip cookies instead of the graham crackers in the recipe she had gotten. "It really became a hit in our church," she said. "Everyone just loves it."

6 cups milk

¾ cup all-purpose flour

2 cups sugar

Pinch of salt

1½ teaspoons vanilla extract

4 large egg yolks

3 cups whipped topping

4 dozen chocolate chip cookies (store-bought, or recipe follows)

Peanut butter, for sandwiching the cookies

Heat 4½ cups of the milk in a large saucepan over medium heat until the milk is scalded (180°F). Whisk in the flour, sugar, salt, vanilla, egg yolks, and the remaining 1½ cups cold milk. Heat the milk mixture until thick, stirring continuously. Remove from the heat and allow to cool.

Fold in the whipped topping. Spread some peanut butter between two chocolate chip cookies to form a cookie sandwich. Repeat until all four dozen cookies have been used. Cut or crumble the cookie sandwiches into the pudding mixture, and stir until well combined.

AMISH COOK SPECIAL RECIPE
BY LOVINA EICHER

OUTRAGEOUS CHOCOLATE CHIP COOKIES
Makes 4 to 5 dozen cookies

This chocolate chip cookie recipe is a favorite of my children and readers. It has appeared in my column on several occasions. It would make a superb cookie to crumble into Flat Rock Pudding (page 59).

2 cups (4 sticks) butter	4 cups all-purpose flour
2 cups granulated sugar	2 cups quick-cooking oats
1½ cups firmly packed brown sugar	4 teaspoons baking soda
2 cups peanut butter	1 teaspoon salt
2 teaspoons vanilla extract	1 (12-ounce) package chocolate chips
4 large eggs, beaten	

Preheat the oven to 350°F.

Melt the butter and mix with the sugars, peanut butter, vanilla, and eggs. Stir until creamy and smooth. Add the flour, oats, baking soda, and salt. Mix the dough until thoroughly blended. Stir in the chocolate chips until evenly distributed throughout the dough. Roll the dough into 1-inch balls and place on baking sheets. Bake the cookies for 10 to 15 minutes, until the edges are golden brown. Transfer to wire racks to cool completely.

SHLICK AND QUICK STRAWBERRY ICE CREAM
Serves 6

Shlick is a Pennsylvania Dutch term for "simple" or "easy," and on a scorching summer day in Flat Rock, Illinois, this refreshing dessert is an amazing antidote to the heat. This unpreserved homemade ice cream will melt faster than commercially sold brands and does not require an ice-cream maker—just stir and freeze. This recipe calls for a product called Clear Jel, which acts as a thickening agent. Clear Jel can be purchased in most bulk food and baking stores. It is a very popular baking and canning ingredient among Amish cooks.

2 cups granulated sugar

¾ cup firmly packed brown sugar

¾ cup instant Clear Jel

½ teaspoon salt

2 to 3 cups heavy cream

2 teaspoons vanilla extract

1 quart frozen, chopped strawberries

3 cups whole milk

Stir the sugars, Clear Jel, and salt in a large mixing bowl. Add the cream, and stir vigorously. Add the vanilla, strawberries, and milk and mix well. Transfer to a freezer-safe container, seal tightly, and freeze until firm.

HOT FUDGE SUNDAE CAKE
Serves 8 to 10

This is good served warm with ice cream or milk. Raw milk is preferred in this settlement. The dessert is cakelike on top, with a nice, warm, syrupy layer beneath.

2 cups all-purpose flour

1½ cups granulated sugar

¾ cup unsweetened cocoa powder

4 teaspoons baking powder

1 teaspoon salt

1 cup milk

¼ cup vegetable oil

2 teaspoons vanilla extract

1 cup walnuts, chopped

1½ cups firmly packed brown sugar

3½ cups boiling water

Preheat the oven to 350°F. Grease a 10 by 15-inch baking pan and set aside.

Sift together the flour, sugar, ½ cup of the cocoa powder, the baking powder, and the salt in a large bowl. Add the milk, vegetable oil, and vanilla, and stir until smooth and well combined. Fold in the nuts until evenly incorporated. Pour the batter into the prepared baking pan, then sprinkle the brown sugar and the remaining ¼ cup cocoa powder on top. Pour the boiling water on top of everything. Bake until the top looks dry, about 40 minutes.

DELICIOUS GREEN BEANS

Serves 4 to 6

Gloria Yoder prefers Roma or Jade green beans. And she has some fond memories from her youth, when she and her sisters would can about 85 quarts a year. "We sat on the ground in a circle and each had a pile of beans in our lap, tossing them into a large bowl in the center," she recalled. "To make time go faster and keep the motivation level higher, we played guessing games, sang, or raced as we worked."

2 pounds green beans, cut up

Salt

3 tablespoons butter

8 ounces bacon, cooked to the desired crispness
    and cut into small pieces

Salt and black pepper

Seasoning salt

Place the green beans in a large pot, cover with water, add salt, and cook until the green beans are tender. Drain.

Melt the butter in a large saucepan over medium heat and cook until browned. Add the green beans to the butter, and stir to coat. Continue to heat until the green beans are steaming hot. Add the cooked bacon, along with salt, and pepper and seasoning salt, and serve.

SCALLOPED CORN

Serves 4 to 6

Illinois is corn country and during the height of summer, fields are filled with rows of towering stalks. Corn is used in casseroles and enjoyed on the cob, slathered with butter. This scalloped corn recipe is also a favorite and is extra tasty when it's made with fresh Silver Queen or sweet corn during the summer.

2 cups fresh or frozen corn kernels

2 large eggs, beaten

1 cup milk

⅔ cup bread or saltine cracker crumbs

1 tablespoon minced onion

3 tablespoons melted butter

½ teaspoon salt

¼ teaspoon black pepper

1 tablespoon sugar

Preheat the oven to 350°F. Lightly grease a 2-quart casserole and set it aside.

Combine all the ingredients in a large mixing bowl and mix until well distributed. Spoon the mixture into the prepared dish. Bake for 40 minutes, until bubbly and golden.

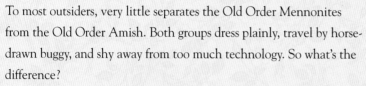

WHO ARE THE OLD ORDER MENNONITES?

To most outsiders, very little separates the Old Order Mennonites from the Old Order Amish. Both groups dress plainly, travel by horse-drawn buggy, and shy away from too much technology. So what's the difference?

Very little, actually. Theologically, the churches are quite similar, and the lifestyles are, too. It's easy to get fooled. Turns out, for instance, that a supposedly wonderful Amish bakery, while certainly wonderful, isn't Amish at all.

This "Amish bakery," the Country Crust Bakery on State Route 41, was in rural, western Ross County, Ohio, and had been there for some time. It was a crisp winter day, and the snow was beginning to swirl with increasing intensity outside. But the slush and snow didn't deter the hardworking bakers at Country Crust, who continued kneading crusts and patting together whoopie pies even as the flakes fell.

"I've heard many great things about this Amish bakery," I said to one of the women behind the counter. She seemed to stifle a slight laugh, as her hands sunk forearm-deep into a bowl of dough.

"You probably should talk to the owner. He's home now, lives around back," the woman said, pointing a flour-covered thumb toward a field. And the owner set things straight: "Let's get one thing straight right away: We aren't Amish," Luke Martin, the bakery owner, said.

He explained that they were Old Order Mennonites. Old Order Mennonite men typically do not wear beards, he said. They do use a horse and buggy, and they dress plainly, so sometimes they can be difficult for uninitiated outsiders to distinguish from Amish. But this was definitely *not* the "Amish bakery near Bainbridge."

Regardless, Country Crust is a great bakery. It offers an assortment of freshly handmade and homemade pies, loaves of bread, pretzels, cream horns, cookies, and whoopie pies that draw people to this rural outpost from miles away, and its tiny batches assure freshness.

The Amish are the best known church whose members rely mainly on the horse and buggy for transportation. But the Old Order Mennonites are a "horse and buggy" church, too, as are a few congregations of Old Order German Baptist Brethren. Just to the north of Sinking Spring, several dozen Old Order Mennonite families call the area home. There's little interaction between the two churches, but they do occasionally attend the produce auction. The quickest way for an outsider to discern whether a buggy is being piloted by an Amish or an Old Order Mennonite, is to look at the male. Old Order Mennonite men traditionally do not grow beards, whereas Amish men do.

RICHARDS, MISSOURI

AT A GLANCE

Date Established: 1997

Church Districts: 1

Culinary highlights: ripe tomatoes, oatmeal bologna, homemade breadsticks

To the non-Amish (and non-Mennonite), it can be difficult to distinguish one from the other (see "Who Are the Old-Order Mennonites?" page 65). One Old Order Mennonite, Misheal Copp, a baker in Richards, Missouri, describes the Amish-Mennonite distinction this way:

"There isn't a lot of difference between the Amish and us. We use horse and buggies only, and use the phone and any modern technology as rarely as possible. Everything is done by horsepower; no motors. We don't tolerate immoral practices and seek to be separated from the world as much as possible."

But there's one strong thing in common between both Old Order Amish and Old Order Mennonites: a love of food. And there are definite differences in tastes between settlements.

In Richards, Missouri, homemade breadsticks, the sort you might find in many restaurants, somehow caught on and are now a must-have by people in the church.

"I tried making them to sell, but they didn't sell like I'd hoped," said Misheal Copp. "The reason? Perhaps others do not enjoy them like our people do," he said. On the other hand, he also said that taco salad, a food that might not be everyone's favorite, is very popular in their settlement.

Fresh produce is a way of life in Richards, as Misheal's sister Arlene described: "Everyone in this community raises produce. Our community started in November 1997 and at first we all lived in a large 'hotel,' as they called it, until the houses were built. There were around five families living in it, and, of course, the children had grand times, but the parents were glad to have their own homes. Here in Missouri, there are two districts [communities]. In Kentucky, there are two; Ohio, one; Indiana, one; and in Belize, two. All raise produce."

She continued, "Watermelons and tomatoes are fun. There are 'pickers,' 'catchers,' and 'labelers.' While the pickers pick, one person throws the tomato or melon to a 'catcher' on the wagon, and young children on the wagon label them. And let's not forget tomato fights. 'Ugh, who gave me that rotten one?' the catcher will yell, and there it goes. Tomatoes—usually rotten ones—are flying thick and fast until Dad says 'Enough!' The definition of *pumpkins* should be 'sore backs,' but really it's interesting family fun to pick the loads and loads, and bins and bins, full of pumpkins. It's especially rewarding when Mom makes the family's favorite pie: pumpkin pie!"

The fresh produce that is so much a part of life in Richards finds its way into even the most everyday foods, such as tomato bread.

TOMATO BREAD

Makes 4 loaves

Misheal Copp says that this is the community's favorite bread for ham and cheese sandwiches. This bread is often served at the after-church meal. Tomatoes are plentiful here in the summer, and this is a great way to use a lot of them. They make the bread in large quantities, but leftover bread can be bagged, sealed, and kept frozen until ready to use.

4½ cups tomato juice

4 tablespoons (½ stick) butter

6 tablespoons sugar

2 tablespoons salt

1 tablespoon ground oregano

1 tablespoon ground basil

½ cup ketchup

3 tablespoons active dry yeast

About 12 cups all-purpose flour

Preheat the oven to 350°F. Grease four standard loaf pans and set aside.

Heat the tomato juice to lukewarm in a large saucepan. Add the butter, sugar, salt, oregano, basil, ketchup, and yeast. Let the mixture sit a few minutes to dissolve the yeast. Stir in enough flour to form a soft dough, kneading when necessary. Let the dough rise in a warm place for 20 minutes. Punch down the dough. Divide the dough among the prepared pans. Allow to rise for 20 minutes longer. Bake for 1 hour.

COOKING FOR A CROWD: OATMEAL BOLOGNA

Large gatherings are a part of Amish and Mennonite life. After-church meals, Sunday evening singings, funerals, weddings, quilting bees, and barn raisings all provide an opportunity for hundreds of people to congregate, mixing work, fellowship, and food. Often Amish and Mennonite kitchen cabinets contain massive mixing bowls, paddle-size spoons, and recipes that could feed a football team or two. This oatmeal bologna recipe is a specialty in Richards, Missouri, and is great served as a sandwich or even fried.

If you are really adventurous or have a large crowd of your own to feed, try this recipe. If not, it can be cut in quantity. The recipe calls for Tender Quick, which is a product made by Morton that can be found in most canning or bulk food stores. It contains potassium nitrate, which serves as a curing agent. Any meat can be used in the recipe, depending on whether you want beef, pork, turkey, or chicken bologna, or you can use a blend of several. Meat can be bought pre-ground from the butcher, but most Amish and Mennonite cooks would grind it themselves.

50 pounds meat, cut off the bones

1 pound Morton's Tender Quick

13 to 14 ounces salt

1 teaspoon saltpeter

2 teaspoons dry mustard

1 teaspoon ground red pepper

2 teaspoons ground mace

1 pound (about 3½ cups) cornstarch

6 teaspoons black pepper

2 cups ground coriander

15 cups quick-cooking oats

½ teaspoon minced garlic

8 to 9 quarts warm water

Bologna casings

Combine the meat, Tender Quick, salt, and saltpeter in a very large container and mix well. Keep cool (42° to 48°F) for 3 days, keeping the container as airtight as possible. After 3 days, combine the dry mustard, red pepper, mace, cornstarch, black pepper, coriander, and oats, and mix well.

Spread the mixture over the meat. Mix well, and run the meat mixture through a grinder once or twice.

Put the ground meat into a large tub. Combine the garlic and 4 quarts of the water until the garlic has dissolved, and pour the garlic mixture over the meat. Add 4 to 5 additional quarts of water, and mix well. Stuff the meat mixture into bologna casings. Place on baking sheets, and bake at 120° to 200°F for 4 to 5 hours, until firmed up. Then cook the bologna in hot water (175° to 200°F) for 1 hour. When done, place the bologna in cold water for 10 minutes to cool. Spread out the rolls until completely cooled, then refrigerate or freeze.

YODER AND HUTCHINSON, KANSAS

YODER

AT A GLANCE

Date established: 1883

Number of church districts: 2

Culinary highlights: Hispanic/traditional

HUTCHINSON

AT A GLANCE

Date established: 1883

Number of church districts: 2

Culinary highlights: Hispanic/traditional foods

Yoder and Hutchinson, Kansas, sit squarely in the center of the Lower 48. For almost a century, this was the end of the line, as far west as the Amish went, so the towns had a frontier feel.

Now, visitors to Yoder and Hutchinson—sitting less than 10 miles apart—can experience the Amish ambiance of a small, self-contained settlement. A good base from which to explore is the Sunflower Inn, a charming bed-and-breakfast that is actually located in a former Amish home and buggy shop. The former Amish owners have since moved to Indiana..

"We get customers from all over the United States, people who are just coming to Yoder to experience the Amish community," said Kendra Horst, who manages the inn and who is herself two generations removed from being Amish.

The inn's Amish ambiance goes right down to the morning wake-up call.

"The rooster wakes you up at six a.m. Some love it, some hate it. Either way, it is nostalgic." Horst laughed.

Of course, as proprietor of an inn, Horst hears many misconceptions about the Amish. "The most common [one] is that the Amish are backward; they only go to school until the eighth grade. But the Amish men know just about as much about current events or politics as anyone," Horst said. "It is a total choice to live the way they do, and you have to respect that."

Yoder Heritage Day is held the fourth Saturday of each August and brings eight to ten thousand people to the tiny village. A big pancake supper benefits the Amish school, as do buggy races that feature two Amish men pulling the buggy, instead of horses.

Yoder and Hutchinson have changed a lot as rural Kansas has experienced an influx of Hispanic residents. Taquerías and cantinas are now as common as corn and cattle. The south-of-the-border culinary influence has seeped into Amish kitchens as well.

Central Kansas features a moderate climate well suited to growing corn and beans. Summers are hot and dry; and winters, cold and windy.

Malinda Yoder, an Amish cook in the Hutchinson settlement, said that the fertile soil of central Kansas is good for growing almost anything. But the plants need a lot more watering than in the rainier climate of the eastern part of the country. Peas can be planted as early as February, with potatoes going in the ground by March. First frost is typically mid-October, with the last frost danger being April 15.

Yoder shared some of her favorite Hutchinson recipes with us, recipes that reflect the area's Hispanic-influenced culinary culture.

FRESH GREEN CHILE SALSA
Makes 2 to 3 cups

Malinda Yoder said she likes to serve this fresh salsa with quesadillas. Homemade salsas are increasingly popular among the Amish because almost everything needed for a tasty version can be grown in one's garden. Amish homemakers discovered salsa was a natural fit onto their menus. Some Amish now make flaming salsas with homegrown jalapeños, while others prefer milder versions. This recipe is great with tortilla chips, crackers, or quesadillas.

3 or 4 Anaheim or poblano peppers, chopped

1½ cups chopped tomatoes

½ cup chopped onion

1 clove garlic, minced

2 tablespoons fresh lime or lemon juice

1 tablespoon snipped fresh cilantro

½ teaspoon salt

⅛ teaspoon ground cumin

Mix together all the ingredients in a medium bowl until well combined. Refrigerate to allow time for the flavors to meld, 30 minutes to 1 hour.

QUESADILLAS

Serves 4 to 6

This is another favorite in the central Kansas Amish settlement, where the Hispanic influence has surged in recent years. Taquerías and Mexican groceries are mainstays in small towns here and they have influenced traditional Kansas cooking.

1 medium onion, finely chopped

¼ cup finely chopped and seeded jalapeño peppers,
    or 2 (4-ounce) cans diced green chiles, drained

2 cups grated sharp Cheddar cheese

2 cups browned beef

10 (8-inch) flour tortillas (page 167)

Fresh Green Chile Salsa (page 70)

Sour cream, for serving

Combine the onion, peppers, cheese, and beef in a medium mixing bowl.

Spray a large skillet or griddle with nonstick spray, and heat over a medium-high flame. Place 1 tortilla in the skillet. Top with ⅔ cup of the cheese mixture, spreading evenly. Top with another tortilla, then cook until the tortilla is lightly browned and the cheese begins to melt, about 1 minute. Carefully flip the tortilla "sandwich" and brown the other side. Decrease the heat slightly, if necessary, to avoid overbrowning. Transfer to a platter and keep warm while you repeat with the remaining tortillas and cheese mixture.

Cut the quesadillas into wedges and spoon the salsa and sour cream on top.

PHEASANT BAKED IN CREAM
Serves 4

Ring-necked pheasant is one of the most popular game birds in Kansas, according to the Kansas Department of Wildlife and Parks. The fowl is a favorite on Amish supper tables.

¼ cup shortening

1 (2½- to 3-pound) pheasant, cut into quarters

1 cup heavy cream or half-and-half, or as needed

¼ cup chopped onion

½ clove garlic, minced

1½ teaspoons Worcestershire sauce

1 teaspoon salt

⅛ teaspoon black pepper

¼ cup cold water

1 tablespoon all-purpose flour

Preheat the oven to 325°F.

Melt the shortening over medium heat in a heavy skillet. Place the pheasant pieces in the pan, and brown the meat on all sides. Transfer the pheasant pieces to a 9 by 13-inch baking dish. Pour the cream over the pheasant, and sprinkle with the onion, garlic, Worcestershire, salt, and pepper.

Cover the dish with foil, crimping the foil to the edge of the dish. Bake for about 2 hours, adding more cream, if necessary, to keep everything moist.

Transfer the pheasant pieces to a serving plate. Strain the cream gravy from the dish into a medium saucepan set over medium heat. Stir together the water and flour in a small bowl. Whisk the flour mixture into the gravy and boil for 1 minute, or until thickened. Serve the pheasant pieces with the gravy.

YODER COFFEECAKE
Serves 4 to 6

Kendra Horst said her Amish grandmother, who was famous in the community for this coffeecake, passed down the recipe, and it is always a huge hit at the Sunflower Inn. Part of its being so good is that she makes it with homemade butter and real vanilla extract.

CAKE

½ cup sugar

1 large egg, beaten

4 tablespoons (½ stick) butter, softened

1½ cups all-purpose flour

3 tablespoons baking powder

¼ teaspoon salt

1 teaspoon vanilla extract

¾ cup whole milk

TOPPING

1 cup firmly packed brown sugar

2 tablespoons all-purpose flour

2 tablespoons ground cinnamon

6 tablespoons melted butter

½ cup chopped walnut pieces

Preheat the oven to 375°F. Grease a 9 by 13-inch baking dish and set it aside.

Mix together the sugar, egg, butter, flour, baking powder, salt, vanilla, and milk in a large mixing bowl. When the mixture has a creamy consistency, spread it into the prepared dish.

Make the topping: Mix all the topping ingredients in a small bowl. Sprinkle over the cake batter. Bake for 20 minutes, or until a toothpick inserted into the center comes out clean.

MY MICHIGAN COMMUNITY

BY LOVINA EICHER

Deer hunting and fishing are very popular in our Michigan community. With Michigan having so many deer and so many fish, a lot of venison and fish can be found on the tables of the local Amish. A lot of fish fries are held for benefits, and freezers are always stocked with fish. During the summer months, you can see a lot of horse and buggies heading to the lakes so people can fish. In the winter, the lakes are the site of a lot of ice fishing so that during the winter months, freezers can once again be stocked. In the fall, deer hunting results in a lot of venison being made into meat loaf, meatballs, chili soup, deer bologna, summer sausage, jerky, and poor man's steak. Grapes, rhubarb, and tea are also easily grown in our areas, so a lot of grape and rhubarb juice is canned. A lot of tea concentrate is made through the winter months. Some folks dry their tea leaves for winter use.

One big difference between this settlement and Berne (see page 88), where I used to live, is that we can have gas-powered appliances here, such as freezers and ovens.

The church lunches are a little different here in Michigan. In Berne, pretty much everyone had ham, bologna, and cheese. Out here, though, someone will have egg salad or cheese spread instead of meat. And in Michigan we have tea, while in Berne they just had coffee after services.

And you can see some differences here in how church services are conducted. When I go to nearby communities, when they have prayer in church, everyone kneels down and is silent. Out in Berne, though, the minister said a prayer out loud. There are small differences in the services from one community to the next. Also we are permitted to have bicycles out here and not in Berne.

A lot of people out here do have their own grapes, and that is one thing that my husband, Joe, would like to get started on. For a good recipe for using some of those grapes, see page 82.

UTICA, MINNESOTA

AT A GLANCE

Date established: 1995

Number of church districts: 3

Culinary highlights: traditional

Minnesota has seen an influx of Amish over the past decade. The state's largest settlement is in the southeast, in Fillmore County, but Amish can now be found statewide, including in some very frigid areas of the far northwest.

As we have seen, Amish cooking and baking are greatly influenced by local flora and fauna, but there are also "old favorites" that get transported to new settlements, and this gives most Amish menus a mix of old and new. An Amish settlement in southeastern Minnesota is a great example.

By early 2011, fifty-four Amish families called the emerald-colored hills of this region home. This is an area of the state known as "bluff country." The Amish worked quickly to weave themselves into the fabric of the Utica community.

In 2009, the Amish started a weekly produce auction held in an old carriage barn. Mom-and-pop grocers compete with buyers from big chain supermarkets and homemakers for fresh, locally grown, pesticide-free produce. Suspender-clad men heave big bags of fresh green beans onto carts as bid cards are waved around in the audience for the Amish auctioneer's attention. The Amish community also holds two large school auctions each year, which attract large crowds of Amish and non-Amish alike.

Utica, Minnesota, features black buggies and basic baking. The local Amish economy has evolved to include furniture and cabinet shops, a bakery, harness shops, a buggy shop, and a tin store. No fewer than thirteen Amish-owned greenhouses have taken root in the fertile soils around Utica.

Sometimes an Amish settlement simply has its tried-and-true favorites. The recipes aren't necessarily a reflection of the local cuisine but are traditions within an area.

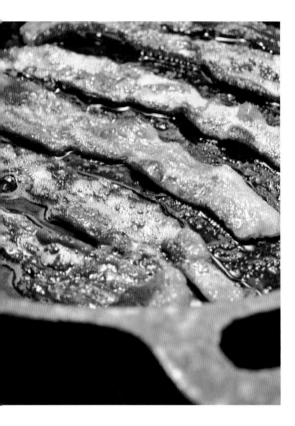

BREAKFAST CASSEROLE
Serves 12

Most Amish cooks have a ready supply of fresh eggs on hand, thanks to the free-range hens that usually roam the property. A breakfast casserole is an excellent—and delicious—way to use some of the supply. This recipe needs overnight refrigeration.

6 slices bread, cubed

3 cups chopped cooked breakfast meat (sausage, bacon, and/or ham)

6 large eggs, beaten

3 tablespoons melted butter

3 cups milk

1 teaspoon dry mustard

1 teaspoon baking powder

8 ounces Colby cheese, shredded

Combine the bread cubes and cooked meat. Place the mixture in a greased 9 by 13-inch pan. Place the eggs, butter, milk, mustard, and baking powder in a mixing bowl, and beat until well combined. Pour the egg mixture into the pan, over the bread and meat.

Cover the dish, and refrigerate the casserole overnight.

Preheat the oven to 325°F.

Bake the casserole for 45 minutes, or until it has firmed up and the top is golden brown. Sprinkle the cheese on top and return to the oven for 3 minutes, to allow the cheese to melt.

PEANUT BUTTER COOKIES
Makes about 2 dozen cookies

This is a classic cookie enjoyed in many Amish settlements. While lard is gradually falling out of favor in Amish kitchens, many still use it, as this cookie recipe reflects.

1 cup lard

1¼ cups granulated sugar

1 cup firmly packed brown sugar

2 large eggs, beaten

1 cup peanut butter

½ teaspoon salt

2 teaspoons baking soda

1½ teaspoons vanilla extract

3 cups all-purpose flour

Preheat the oven to 350°F.

Cream together the lard, 1 cup of the granulated sugar, and the brown sugar in a large bowl until light and fluffy. Mix in the eggs, peanut butter, salt, baking soda, vanilla, and flour, stirring until well combined. Form the dough into 1-inch balls, then roll the balls in the reserved ¼ cup granulated sugar. Place the balls on baking sheets, flattening slightly. Bake until the cookies are browned at the edges, 10 to 12 minutes.

FERTILE, MINNESOTA

AT A GLANCE

Date established: 2007

Number of church districts: 1

Culinary highlights: chokecherries, garden huckleberries

In 2012, thirteen families called this aptly named small town 50 miles southeast of Grand Forks, North Dakota, home. This area is known for being plunged into brutal deep freezes during winter and experiencing merciless blizzards, so the growing season is shorter than in most areas popular with the Amish. But the Amish who moved here are hearty.

"We laugh at Southerners' fear of our winters. At least we need not fear ice storms or poisonous snakes, although we do sometimes have blizzards and tornadoes," said William Bontrager, one of the first Amish farmers who moved here. He added that the growing season isn't as short as one might expect. "The first killing frost often comes about the same time as it does in Missouri, but the spring does usually come much later." The deep snow and cold make self-sufficiency paramount during the long winter.

"It should be the rule to have the winter's supply of wood on hand by October or November, as the snow can get so deep it's almost impossible to cut wood in the woods by then," Bontrager said.

The culinary highlight of the summer in the Fertile community are the chokecherries that grow in abundance along fencerows in the area. The plant can reach as high as 20 feet.

"We often bend them down to pick the upper branches or else leave them for the birds, as the trees are rarely big enough to climb. For the best flavor, they should be picked once they are black but still have a shiny look, as the flavor is not as good once they are overripe," Bontrager remarked.

The chokecherries are harvested in buckets and brought back home, where they are prepared for storage.

"We usually stuff the cherries into jars and cover with water and water-bath them, boiling for twenty minutes. When we want to eat them, we dump a jar into a cheese colander and mash the cherries with our hands, rinsing out as much pulp and juice until the leftovers look a little whitish. Usually one quart of cherries has enough flavor to make three cups of juice ready for pie filling, tapioca, or mush," Bontrager said.

Another summer delicacy in the Fertile area are garden huckleberries, which are not related to the huckleberries found in St. Ignatius, Montana (see page 157). The garden huckleberry is more closely related to a tomato and is cultivated, because they fare well in northern Minnesota's climate.

"It is the most purple food I have ever seen, if processed at the right stage and not overcooked," Bontrager said. The seeds should be started indoors and handled like tomatoes.

"We don't usually harvest them until right before the first frost. They are a low-growing plant with branches covered with clusters of dime-size purple fruit once ripe. It is easiest to clip off the branches and carry them to the convenient place to pick the berries off," Bontrager noted. He also described how they use both chokecherries and garden huckleberries in similar recipes.

"For both of these fruits, we sometimes add vanilla or lemon juice to enhance the flavor. We prefer the chokecherry to the huckleberry, but other families here prefer the huckleberry," Bontrager said.

CHOKECHERRY TAPIOCA
Serves 15 to 20

You won't see tapioca this colorful very often. The chokecherries color the dish, so if you're used to plain, pearl tapioca, this will be a change! Add lemon juice while the mixture is boiling, if you get it too sweet. Sliced apples or fresh or canned fruit may be mixed with the tapioca when it is cold, plus whipped cream if desired. Adding sugar after it is done cooking keeps it from getting stringy.

2 quarts prepared chokecherry juice

¼ teaspoon salt

1¼ cups baby pearl tapioca

½ cup sugar, or to taste

2 teaspoons vanilla or almond extract

In a large saucepan, mix the juice, salt, and tapioca. Bring to a boil over medium-high heat and cook at a boil for about 15 minutes, stirring constantly, until the tapioca is clear. Turn down the heat and simmer for another 20 minutes, then remove from the heat and let cool to room temperature. Stir in the sugar and vanilla, and refrigerate overnight before serving.

CHOKECHERRY MUSH
Serves 10

This is a favorite in Fertile, and a local twist on a classic dish. The mush is livened up even more by adding a splash of lemon juice or vanilla. It tastes good with cornbread or milk. Perma-Flow is a thickener similar to Clear Jel.

3 quarts prepared chokecherry juice

1 cup Perma-Flow thickener

1 cup sugar

¼ cup water

Combine the chokecherry juice, Perma-Flow thickener, sugar, and water in a saucepan over medium heat. Cook for 5 minutes, stirring constantly, until thickened. Remove from the heat and serve hot.

GARDEN HUCKLEBERRY PIE
Makes one 9-inch pie

Unlike wild huckleberries out west, garden huckleberries can be grown in the garden, although they are still often just picked wild around here. Garden huckleberries are very tart, and most people don't like them that way; but when they're used in a pie, bread, or jam, the flavor really comes out.

1 quart prepared garden huckleberry juice

½ cup cornstarch

½ cup sugar

1 (9-inch) prebaked pie shell

Whipped cream, for topping

Combine the huckleberry juice, cornstarch, and sugar in a small saucepan over medium heat and cook, stirring constantly, until thickened. Let cool. Pour the mixture into the baked pie shell and top with whipped cream before serving.

AMISH COOK SPECIAL RECIPE
BY LOVINA EICHER

HOMEMADE GRAPE SALAD
Serves 12 to 15

The Amish often serve this with dinner. It's a refreshing dish that's great in the summer when you don't want to heat up the kitchen. This is not something that was served in Indiana, but it is popular here in Michigan.

8 ounces cream cheese, softened

1½ cups powdered sugar

1 cup sour cream

1 teaspoon fresh lemon juice

4 pounds red or green seedless grapes, halved

1 cup crushed pineapple, drained

8 ounces whipped topping, such as Cool Whip

Beat together the cream cheese, sugar, sour cream, and lemon juice in a large bowl, until smooth and creamy. Fold in the grapes, pineapple, and whipped topping, then serve.

KINGSTON, WISCONSIN

AT A GLANCE

Date established: 1995

Number of church districts: 2

Culinary highlights: blue cheese

The Amish have had a long presence in Wisconsin. Throughout most of the state's history, the population has been small, relegated to a few enclaves in the central and southern parts of the state. But even though their presence historically has been minimal, the Wisconsin Amish have made their mark.

It was, in fact, a Wisconsin settlement that challenged longstanding state and federal laws regarding compulsory education. A landmark Supreme Court case, *Yoder vs. Wisconsin*, ultimately enshrined the Amish right to educate their children as they see fit, which means to the eighth grade. That battle took place near the town of New Glarus, in the southern part of the state.

In ruling for the Amish, Chief Justice Warren Burger summed up Amish life eloquently. His words ring as true today as they did when the ruling was issued in 1972:

> *Amish objection to formal education beyond the eighth grade is firmly grounded in these central religious concepts. They object to the high school, and higher education generally, because the values they teach are in marked variance with Amish values and the Amish way of life; they view secondary school education as an impermissible exposure of their children to a "worldly" influence in conflict with their beliefs.*

The 1990s saw the Amish population surge in Wisconsin, as many saw the state's plentiful and reasonably priced land and the *Yoder* case as a beacon. Wisconsin is the land of the Green Bay Packers and cheese. And while the Amish have been slow to embrace the former (baseball has always been an Amish pastime), they have become ardent adherents of the latter. Nowhere have the Amish found their dairy niche more than around the community of Cambria, where the Salemville Cheese Factory makes deliciously crafted cheese. The Salemville Cheese Co-op is the only entirely Old Order Amish–run cheese factory in the United States. The first hint that this place was different was the employee parking lot, which didn't have any cars, just horse-drawn buggies. Adding to the factory's "plain" presence was the small on-site retail store, which sells a variety of cheeses and was staffed solely by Amish workers.

Salemville's cheese niche is narrow: The company makes only blue cheese and one variant, Gorgonzola cheese. It seems like there isn't much middle ground when it comes to blue cheese: You either love it or you hate it. Many Amish in central Wisconsin have learned to love it. More than sixty Amish dairy farmers participate in the unique co-op that supplies the milk to the Salemville Cheese Company. Amish participating in the co-op hand-milk their cows twice a day and deliver the milk to the Salemville Cheese Company in 10-gallon containers.

LaVerne Miller, who manages the property, arrived there with one of several groups of Amish that have settled in central Wisconsin from northern Indiana. Prior to moving to Wisconsin, he had no prior experience with blue cheese.

"They are both mold-ripened cheeses, but Gorgonzola is an older cheese," Miller explained. The Gorgonzola cheese has to age for 90 days, while regular blue cheese ages for 60. The aroma inside the tiny, nondescript cheese factory is that of an overpowering wave of blue cheese.

"When we started out in 1984, we would use nine thousand pounds of milk," LaVerne said, describing the annual milk usage. Almost thirty years later, Salemville uses three times that amount. He explained that a lot of the process to perfection has been trial and error.

"A lot of things we had to learn the hard way," LaVerne said. For fifteen years, Miller, his wife, and their growing young family inhabited the relatively cramped living quarters above the cheese factory, unusual living arrangements for most Amish, who tend to live on spacious lots. Now Miller and his family live on a nearby farm.

Miller is a certified cheese maker. Five Amish sit on the board of directors of the cheese co-op, which guides the business. Salemville cheese is found in many major retailers, including Kroger and Costco.

So what is Miller's favorite way to enjoy blue cheese?

"It goes well with fruit. I love to eat it with an apple," he said. He, like many Amish from northern Indiana, wasn't always a blue cheese fan.

"It took me a while, but I like it," Miller said.

Miller guides visitors through the cheese-making operation— even to the point of donning a covering for his beard. It's fascinating to watch the cheese born from its liquefied milky mass sloshing around in vats, brought to its final form in the aging process, and then as it's crumbled into fine blue cheese. This whole process takes time, and a lot of science is involved. One entire room is devoted to aging the cheeses for 60 to 90 days, depending on the variety. At this point in the production process, the cheese has been shaped into large cylinder-shaped blocks. And there they sit, awaiting their turn to be set free and turned into finely marbled crumbles, which will then find their way onto people's potatoes, salads, and fruits.

Here are some of the delicious blue cheese recipes procured from this charming Central Wisconsin community.

BLUE CHEESE DRESSING OR DIP

Makes about 1½ cups

This dressing can be used on salad or as a dip for vegetables or hot wings. It is a creamy dip with decadent chunks of blue cheese buried in it.

¾ cup sour cream

¼ cup mayonnaise

1½ teaspoons chopped fresh dill

2 ounces blue cheese, crumbled

Whisk together the sour cream and mayonnaise in a small mixing bowl until creamy and well blended. Add the dill and blue cheese and stir to combine. The dressing is ready to serve, or may be chilled first.

BEEF AND BLUE CHEESE SUPPER
Serves 4 to 6

This is a hearty, delicious dish that melds meat, potatoes, and the flavor of blue cheese. Homegrown tomatoes are plentiful in the warm Wisconsin summer, and they are incorporated flavorfully into this dish to make it a complete meal.

4 medium-size russet potatoes

Butter, for dressing the potatoes

Sour cream, for dressing the potatoes

Salt and black pepper, for seasoning

2 (6-ounce) beef tenderloin fillets, 1½ inches thick

1 large tomato, diced

3 green onions, sliced

3 ounces blue cheese, crumbled

Pierce the potatoes with a fork and bake for about 1 hour at 375°F, or microwave them on HIGH for 12 minutes, or until they reach your desired doneness. Cut a slit in each potato and fluff the insides with a fork. Season each potato lightly with your preferred amount of butter, sour cream, and salt and pepper.

While the potatoes are cooking, grill the steak to your desired doneness. Cut the cooked steak into bite-size pieces and place equal amounts in each potato. Sprinkle the potatoes with the tomato, green onions, and blue cheese.

BLUE CHEESE AND CHIVE MASHED POTATOES
Serves 6 to 8

Here's a delicious blue cheesy, chive-y potato dish that creates a wonderful array of flavors.

2 pounds russet potatoes, peeled and cut into 1½-inch chunks

½ cup crumbled blue cheese

4 tablespoons (½ stick) butter

¼ cup snipped fresh chives

½ teaspoon garlic salt

¼ teaspoon black pepper

Cook the potato chunks in boiling water in a medium saucepot until they are fork-tender, 15 to 20 minutes. Drain the potatoes well, return them to the pot, and mash them with a potato masher until smooth. Stir in the blue cheese, butter, chives, garlic salt, and pepper until thoroughly combined. Return the mashed potatoes to the stove and cook for a few minutes more, until very hot.

WHO ARE THE SWISS AMISH?

The Swiss influence is powerful in some Midwestern Amish settlements. In a quiet corner of Indiana, tucked along US 27, observant travelers may notice that they're passing through towns that share the same names as those in Switzerland. Berne and nearby Geneva, Indiana, both nurture strong ties to their Swiss namesakes. Many of the towns' earlier inhabitants were Swiss Mennonites, but Amish from the same regions also settled in the surrounding swampland and farmland that make up the headwater region of the Wabash River. The Amish here differ from Amish elsewhere in some subtle and some noticeable ways.

Perhaps the most noticeable difference is the absence of any covered buggies. All buggies in this area are uncovered or are, as some locals jokingly call them, "topless buggies." This can be pleasant on a temperate spring day, but brutal on an icy January morning or during a drenching summer thunderstorm. The tradition of the topless buggy endures, but few people know why anymore. One explanation about the origins of the topless buggy dates back to the 1700s. Some speculate that the covered buggies closely resembled the early covered carriages that symbolized wealth and status, especially among the English aristocracy, and the conservative Amish around Berne wanted to avoid being associated with that.

Another key difference found among the Swiss Amish is the dialect. They speak a rare, vanishing dialect of Bernese Swiss, while most other Amish speak a dialect of Pennsylvania German (often referred to as Pennsylvania Dutch). The two dialects are so distinctive and different that Amish living just down Route 27 around Fountain City, Indiana, have difficulty understanding the language. The several thousand Amish who inhabit Adams County, Indiana, also practice the art of yodeling. It's enchanting and haunting. The yodeling tells stories through song. Cold winter evenings are often whiled away yodeling. Even the youngest chime in, too, as the custom is passed down, safe for yet another generation.

Other differences are more subtle, such as the use of celery—serving purely a decorative purpose—on the table at Swiss Amish weddings. Celery isn't incorporated at all in other Amish weddings.

Some speculate that the celery somehow symbolizes fertility, but like many Amish traditions its true origin has been lost to history.

The Swiss Amish of Berne have established several other satellite settlements, or daughter communities as they are sometimes called, in Milroy, Indiana; Hudson, Kentucky; and Seymour, Missouri. In all of these places, the same uncovered buggies, yodeling, and Swiss language can also be found. Swiss surnames such as Graber, Hilty, and Schwartz are common.

The Swiss influence also extends to the food. Foods popular among the Amish in Adams County are not embraced elsewhere. The following recipes are a few popular Swiss Amish foods.

RIVEL SOUP

Serves 6 to 8

This is a common soup in the Berne, Indiana, community, and a very typical meal scratched out of whatever is in the pantry. The title refers to the small rounds of dough that you'll find in the soup.

8 cups chicken broth
2 cups all-purpose flour
1 teaspoon salt
2 large eggs, beaten
1 onion, diced
2 tablespoons dried parsley
2 (14.5-ounce) cans of corn or equivalent amount of home-canned
2 cups cooked, diced chicken (optional)

Bring the broth to a boil in a large pot over medium heat. In a large mixing bowl, mix the flour, salt, and eggs to form a crumbly mixture. Rub the mixture between your fingers over the broth, dropping in pea-size pellets, or rivels.

Add the onion, parsley, and corn, and cook until the vegetables are tender, 10 to 15 minutes. If you choose, add the chicken just before you take the soup off the stove.

PON HOSS
Serves 12

This recipe is always made in large quantities. Hog butchering is only done once or twice a year, and when processing a 300-pound porker, you get a lot of meat. Some people refer to this dish by its more common name: scrapple. The Amish in Indiana and points west spell it "Pon Hoss," as the spelling has evolved phonetically. The Amish of Pennsylvania and other eastern states still write it by its more familiar German spelling: "Pon Haus". This dish does require setting overnight, so start the day before you want to eat it.

3 to 4 pounds pork shanks or hocks
About 4 cups of cornmeal or flour for every gallon of broth
2 tablespoons salt for every gallon of broth
1 tablespoon pepper for every gallon of broth

Cook the pork in a large pot over medium heat until tender, about 30 minutes. As the meat cooks, it will make its own broth. Transfer the meat to a plate to cool. Once cool enough to handle, remove the bones from the meat and skim the fat from the broth. Return the meat to the broth and add just enough cornmeal or flour to thicken the liquid to a thin paste. The exact amount will vary, depending on the meat used and the amount of broth, so add the flour 1 cup at a time. Season with salt and pepper.

Pour the mixture into loaf pans. Cover and chill overnight. To serve, slice the chilled meat and fry in a large skillet over medium-high heat until golden brown on each side.

NOTHINGS

Makes 8 pastries

This is a pastry commonly served as a dessert at weddings in the Swiss communities. The dish is decorative and functional. The Nothings are stacked on plates and placed on tables for guests to enjoy after a hearty meal.

1 large egg

¾ cup heavy cream

Pinch of salt

2 to 3 cups all-purpose flour

Lard or shortening, such as Crisco, for frying

Powdered sugar, for sprinkling

Place the egg in a large mixing bowl and beat until foamy. Stir in the cream, salt, and enough flour to form a stiff dough. Knead the dough until well combined, then divide the dough into eight balls.

On a floured work surface, roll out each ball of dough into a very thin circle. Cut three slits into each flat piece of dough.

Place the lard in a large skillet and heat until ready for frying. One by one, fry each piece of dough, turning once, until golden on both sides. Remove from the hot oil, set on paper towels to cool, and then sprinkle the pastry with powdered sugar. Stack the finished pastries on a serving plate.

THE AMISH ECONOMY

Historically, the Amish were an agrarian society, earning their living and drawing their life from the land. Amish culture was built around the farmstead, which preserved their way of life and family units in a way that few other professions could. While the Amish remained on the farm, their lives changed little as automobiles and airplanes and suburban sprawl began to swirl around them.

Beginning in the mid-nineteenth century, several factors converged and began to make agriculture an increasingly difficult way to make a living. Foremost among those factors was the large size of the typical Amish family. Eight, nine, ten, children are quite common among the Amish, and it simply wasn't economically possible for this increasing Amish population to all make their living off the land. Amish men are primarily viewed as the breadwinners in this still-gender-defined culture. So it was Amish men who began to venture from the fields and into the factories in some places. In the nation's third largest Amish settlement—in northern Indiana—about the same time the Amish were leaving farming, the rest of America was discovering recreation vehicles. The combination of northern Indiana's large Amish population, the pool of willing workers, and the factories' need for labor, made for a marriage that lasted decades. But when the Great Recession of 2008 hit, the Amish realized their vulnerability, and many found themselves unemployed for the first time in their lives.

While the Amish of northern Indiana were tossed into unemployment on a large scale for the first time in their history, some didn't view it as a terrible thing in the long term.

"We used to not depend so much on factory work. Our fathers never did. So maybe this is a good thing. It's forcing us to be more creative, to return to our roots, to be more self-sufficient. I'm sharpening lawn mower blades, selling milk, starting a greenhouse; and my wife has doubled the size of her garden so she can start a produce stand," said one Berne, Indiana, Amish man who had been laid off from one of the factories. Like many Amish, he declined to give his name for inclusion in a print interview.

Elsewhere, home-based businesses have been the mainstay of Amish employment. Furniture making and cabinet making, sawmills, pallet making, and canvas shops all have become popular "micro-businesses" among the Amish. Home-based businesses allow the Amish to preserve their family life while still earning an income.

Yet some Amish seem to be testing the bounds of entrepreneurial aspirations among their fellow Amish. For example, an Amish man in Pennsylvania bought a potato chip company. And it's not just men. Amish women have increasingly been showing entrepreneurial streaks. Elizabeth Coblentz was something of a trailblazer when she began writing "The Amish Cook" column in 1991. There are now several widely published Old Order Amish authors. In Illinois, two Amish women opened a coffee and espresso bar, complete with a drive-through. "Would you like a latte with that?" is not something you'd typically expect an Amish person to ask!

NAVARRE, OHIO

AT A GLANCE

Date established: 1910

Number of church districts: 227 in surrounding Stark, Holmes, and Wayne Counties

Culinary highlights: traditional, Ohio dairy and garden

The Amish settlement at Navarre, Ohio, a little town on the banks of the Tuscarawas River, rests on the northern edge of the world's largest concentration of "plain people." Navarre was founded in 1834 and grew quickly with the arrival of the Ohio & Erie Canal, which remained in use until a devastating flood in 1913.

A quaint throwback to small-town America, the village is infused with a sense of beauty and history. Navarre has many small shops downtown, where buggies are almost as common as cars. Visitors can also take a trip along a historic pathway that follows the Tuscarawas River through the village and township and into Amish Country to the south, where the emerald hills are dotted with Amish selling baked goods, and produce and operating other home-based businesses. The Amish at Navarre also take advantage of Ohio's superb garden climate to create a bounty of fresh vegetable salads.

MOIST CHOCOLATE CAKE
Serves 14 to 16

This is an easy chocolate cake, typical of many Amish "from-the-pantry" desserts. It goes great with a scoop of vanilla ice cream.

3 cups all-purpose flour

2 cups sugar

¼ cup unsweetened cocoa powder

2 teaspoons baking soda

1 teaspoon salt

1 cup vegetable oil

2 tablespoons white vinegar

1 teaspoon vanilla extract

2 cups water

Preheat the oven to 350°F.

Sift together the flour, sugar, cocoa, baking soda, and salt into a large bowl. Add the oil, vinegar, vanilla, and water and stir to form a smooth batter. Pour the batter into a greased 9 by 13-inch baking pan and bake until a toothpick inserted in the center comes out clean, 30 to 40 minutes.

HOMEMADE BROCCOLI SALAD
Serves 10 to 12

This salad is a crunchy collision of sweet and savory, perfect in a larger quantity for a party or picnic.

1 head broccoli, chopped	½ cup sugar
1 head cauliflower, chopped	½ teaspoon salt
1 cup mayonnaise	8 ounces bacon, fried and crumbled
1 cup sour cream	1 cup shredded Cheddar cheese

Combine the chopped broccoli and cauliflower in a large bowl. In a separate bowl, combine the mayonnaise, sour cream, sugar, and salt to make a creamy dressing. Add the dressing to the vegetables, stirring to evenly coat. Stir in the bacon and ¾ cup of the cheese. Sprinkle the remaining ¼ cup cheese on top and serve.

JUST-RIGHT CUSTARD PIE

Makes one 9-inch pie

This is a classic, traditional Amish recipe that creates a light, fluffy pie. This can also be enjoyed for breakfast.

2 large eggs, separated

¾ cup sugar

2 tablespoons all-purpose flour

Pinch of salt

2 cups milk, scalded

1 teaspoon vanilla extract

1 (9-inch) unbaked pie shell (see Never-Fail Pastry, page 24)

Preheat the oven to 400°F.

Beat the egg yolks in a bowl, then stir in the sugar, flour, and salt. Very gradually, add the heated milk to the egg yolk mixture.

In a separate bowl, beat the egg whites and vanilla until foamy. Add to the milk mixture, and stir until evenly combined.

Pour the custard into the pie shell, and bake for 10 minutes. Decrease the oven temperature to 325°F and bake until nicely browned on top, about 25 minutes.

THE AMISH COOK'S MIDWESTERN OBSERVATIONS

BY LOVINA EICHER

The foods in this chapter are familiar, since this is where we live. But even between settlements in the Midwest there are differences in food to be found. For instance, venison is more common here than where we used to live in Indiana. Egg salad is more popular here than where I lived in Indiana, too.

Blueberries are really popular around here, so much so that we pick our own, although it sounds like they are even more plentiful in the Amish communities of Maine (see page 14). I've also heard of people here canning the juice from blackberries, kind of similar to how we make rhubarb juice.

AMISH COOKS ACROSS THE
SOUTH

The Amish have been slow to settle the U.S. South, choosing even far-flung western locales over closer Dixie states. The one Southern exception has been Kentucky, which beginning in the mid-1990s started seeing thousands of Amish arrivals from Pennsylvania and Ohio. The temperate climate, fertile soil, and less touristy environment made the Bluegrass State appealing. Tennessee has also had an Amish presence for some time, mainly in the central part of the state, near Ethridge (see page 107).

Amish cooking has, over time, taken on a Southern flair, with cornbread, pork and beans, pecan pie, and okra becoming staples on menus. Plants native to the South, such as muscadines and peanuts, have also been incorporated into cooking.

Because the Amish don't have electricity, air-conditioning is not an option, and that makes the sweltering South unappealing for many. The climate, the clay-packed soil, and cultural differences have also long acted as a deterrent to Amish settlement of the South. But that now seems to be changing. Amish families have settled in some of the southern bayous of Arkansas and the piney hills of northern Mississippi, and a handful of Amish communities can now be found in rural parts of the Carolinas.

One Southern community is so far south that it is almost north. Pinecraft, Florida, which serves as a winter way station for Amish looking to escape the brutal blizzards and cold of the Midwest, often has more people from Ohio and Indiana living there than actual Floridians.

Perhaps the most ambitious attempt to start a Southern settlement can be found in an area more known for its taquerías and javelinas than for buggies and bonnets. This settlement, just outside Beeville, Texas, is far closer to Mexico than it is to any other Amish community. We'll begin there.

BEEVILLE, TEXAS

AT A GLANCE

Date established: 1997

Number of church districts: 1

Culinary highlights: jalapeños, okra

An arid wind blows across the rural Texas prairie only about 200 miles from the border with Mexico. There's a lonely beauty to this corner of Texas, where tumbleweeds and cactus are more common than oaks and elms. Coyotes and javelinas (wild pigs native to the area) prowl the prairie. There's almost always a breeze that tempers the scorching South Texas sun, and the air is drier, devoid of the heavy humidity that soaks the South elsewhere. Several hundred miles to the south, across the Rio Grande, Old Order Mennonites have carved a large community in similar lands. But here the Amish are just getting their start, trying to build something lasting in the least likely of places.

The arid plains of South Texas aren't the first place that comes to mind when one thinks of the Amish. So locals in Beeville were surprised one day in 1997 when the Department of Transportation began erecting the yellow signs warning of slow-moving buggies and horse-drawn carriages selling produce and baked goods began appearing at the local farmers' market. And now buggies clatter down Gaitan Lane, a reminder that one has entered the only Amish enclave for 500 miles or more in any direction.

The small settlement of Amish outside of Beeville was the brainchild of Truman Borntrager, the community's bishop, who discovered the area when he passed through on his way to Mexico to buy produce for a business he ran in Tennessee. While Amish don't drive automobiles, many of them practice astute entrepreneurial skills. Hiring a driver to take them places, as Borntrager did, is not off-limits.

The Amish outside of Beeville scratch out a living by selling produce, beekeeping, and operating some home-based businesses, such as greenhouses, herb sales, and on-site horse training.

In the ten years following his arrival, Borntrager and his family turned a barren tract of South Texas scrubland into an unlikely Garden of Eden. Citing a curative climate of almost nonstop arid breezes and constant sunshine as his main reason for moving here, Borntrager has managed to inadvertently create an interesting Amish culinary fusion— Tex-Mex meets Mediterranean meets traditional Amish cooking.

Truman Borntrager runs the Combination Shop, which, as its name implies, sells a little bit of everything, though it specializes in making buggies and carriages and marketing them to non-Amish customers. It serves as the hub of this small settlement. The highlight for locals is the fresh baked goods on Fridays. Apple, cherry, buttermilk, and pecan pies are favorites, as are cinnamon rolls and banana-nut bread.

Borntrager lives across Gaitan Lane on a huge tract of land dotted with thick groves of citrus trees and fresh figs. If you're ever standing by an orange tree, pick an orange and taste the difference between a fresh-off-the-tree fruit and the often rubbery, bland fruits sometimes found in stores.

Anyone expecting Lancaster County South at Beeville will come away disappointed. The Amish here keep to themselves and don't like a lot of attention, although that changed one winter afternoon in 2010, when Amish farmer John Borntrager, one of Truman's sons, spotted a rare bird, a northern wheatear, on his farm. Bird-watching is a favorite pastime among the Amish. The wheatear spotted in 2010 was only the second recorded sighting of the small bird typically found only in the Arctic. Soon the Borntrager farm was a magnet for birders from across the South, some of whom drove hundreds of miles. The entrepreneurial spirit soon showed itself and the Borntragers had set up a table offering homemade pecan brittle, peanut brittle, and produce for sale.

As the sunrise bathes the Texas scrubland with a serene quiet unlike what you'll find almost anywhere else, John Borntrager is up at five a.m., eating a typical breakfast of cornmeal mush, pancakes, fried potatoes, zucchini, and yellow squash fried with eggs. John and his wife usually eat fresh vegetables three times a day. Supper might consist of bread, peanut butter, jelly, pickles, red beets, tomatoes, and greens.

John Borntrager has had to work to make the rocky South Texas soil arable, but he's seeing results. He uses an arsenal of organic

remedies to help create a fertile soil conducive to bountiful produce. He adds blackstrap molasses to the soil, providing a carbohydrate buffet for a wide variety of beneficial microorganisms. Other pests that Amish farmers farther north don't have to deal with include fire ants, which he'll combat with magnesium and Epsom salt. The results of his and others' efforts in the community have led to a business that supplies local grocery chains with locally grown produce.

A dozen Amish families call the Beeville area home. As in most other Amish communities, church services rotate between the homes of family members. A small school on one of the Amish properties provides for the educational needs of the children. Their relatively young settlement provides a case study in the evolution of local Amish culinary culture. Jalapeños, figs, masa flour, olives, and okra vie for space on the supper table alongside such traditional Amish favorites as homemade buttered noodles and beef stew. Other distinctly Mexican favorites, such as tatume squash and chili patins, are also being embraced by the Amish who have moved here.

Homegrown lemons are used in lemon puddings, pies, and lemonade. Wild grapes grow and are turned into jellies. However, apples, such a popular food in other Amish settlements, don't do too well in South Texas.

"Apples need chill hours," John Borntrager said.

OKRA GUMBO

Serves 4 to 6

You can substitute other meats on hand for the sausage. Unlike typical gumbos found elsewhere in the South, this Amish adaptation does not begin with a roux and end with hours of stovetop simmering.

1 tablespoon vegetable oil

8 ounces smoked sausage, casing removed and cut in ½-inch-thick slices

4 cups sliced okra

1 green bell pepper, seeded and chopped

1 medium-size onion, chopped

2 cloves garlic, minced

3 medium-size tomatoes, peeled and chopped

Salt and black pepper

Cooked rice, for serving (optional)

Heat the vegetable oil over medium heat in a Dutch oven. Add the sausage and cook, stirring occasionally, until browned, 3 to 4 minutes. Remove the browned sausage with a slotted spoon, and set aside.

Add the okra, green pepper, onion, and garlic to the Dutch oven, and sauté in the reserved pan drippings until tender. Add the chopped tomatoes and the reserved sausage. Decrease the heat to medium-low, and simmer for 30 minutes, stirring frequently. Season with salt and pepper to taste. The gumbo may be served over cooked rice, if desired.

PICKLED OKRA

Makes 10 to 12 pints

Okra grows very well in the arid soils of southern Texas and is a staple in most Amish gardens. Okra is served almost every night for supper when it is in season, and the Amish frequently prepare for okra's off-season by canning a large quantity and saving it for later use.

8 to 9 pounds fresh okra pods, washed and trimmed

10 to 12 cloves garlic

¾ cup canning or pickling salt

3 quarts water

1 quart white vinegar

2 tablespoons dill seeds

Pack the okra into hot, sterilized, pint-size canning jars. For this quantity of okra, plan on ten to twelve jars. Add one whole clove of garlic to each jar of okra.

Place the canning or pickling salt, water, vinegar, and dill seeds in a large, nonreactive pot and bring the solution to a boil. Using a funnel, pour the pickling solution into each jar of okra, leaving ¼ to ½ inch of headspace.

Apply the warm, sterilized lids and bands to the canning jars, and place them in a boiling water bath for 10 minutes. Remove the jars from the water bath and allow them to cool. Check the jars after they have cooled to make sure the lids have sealed. Wait approximately 1 week before using.

SOUTH TEXAS RICE
Serves 6 to 8

This is a one-pot dish that melds some of the most powerful flavors of the Rio Grande region with such traditional Amish staples as hamburger and tomatoes.

8 ounces ground beef

1 green bell pepper, seeded and
    cut into medium dice

1 red bell pepper, seeded and
    cut into medium dice

1 large onion, finely chopped

1 jalapeño pepper, seeded and chopped

2 cups uncooked white rice

4 cups tomato juice

1 to 2 teaspoons taco seasoning

1 teaspoon chili seasoning mix

2 teaspoons garlic powder

2 teaspoons salt

1 to 2 teaspoons fajita seasoning

1 tomato, chopped

1 teaspoon dried basil

In a very large skillet or Dutch oven, brown the hamburger meat, green and red peppers, and onion. Drain off the grease, then add the jalapeño, rice, tomato juice, taco seasoning, chili seasoning mix, garlic powder, salt, fajita seasoning, tomato, and basil, and stir until thoroughly mixed.

Bring the mixture to a boil over medium-high heat, decrease the heat to low, and cover the skillet. Allow the mixture to simmer until the rice is tender and has absorbed most of the liquid, about 30 minutes.

HOMEMADE YOGURT
Serves 16

Homemade yogurt can be used in a variety of ways, and this is an easy, from-scratch formula. Yogurt is great served with homemade granola and can be substituted in almost any recipe that calls for mayonnaise or sour cream. Homemade yogurt spooned over a baked potato is another popular use. The yogurt can even be strained to make into "yogurt cheese," which is spreadable like cream cheese. Most Amish cooks use raw (unpasteurized) milk for this recipe, but it can be made with store-bought pasteurized milk. Whole milk should be used, though, because lower-fat milks can cause a runnier yogurt. Also, the sugar can be omitted for a less sweet variation. Finally, the Amish use leftover yogurt from a previous batch for the culture. If this is your first batch, you can use plain store-bought yogurt. Just make sure it doesn't have any added ingredients and includes live, active cultures.

1 gallon whole milk

2 cups active culture yogurt

½ cup sugar

Flavorings and additions, such as vanilla, fruit, and honey, as desired

Heat the milk to between 170° and 180°F. Do not allow the milk to boil. Add the active culture yogurt and the sugar, and stir with a wire whisk until the sugar is dissolved. You may also add any desired flavorings at this point. Allow the milk to cool to 120°F.

Preheat the oven to 100°F. If your oven cannot be set that low, set it to its lowest setting for 10 minutes, then turn it off. It should stay warm for 12 hours if left closed. If you open the oven door, reheat the oven for about 30 seconds to maintain temperature.

Pour the milk into a jug or a glass container and wrap the container with a bath towel to maintain temperature. Place it in the preheated oven and let it sit overnight.

Remove the container from the oven and save 2 cups of the yogurt for use in your next batch. You can serve the remaining yogurt warm or chilled. For thicker yogurt, strain it through cheesecloth. For yogurt cheese, wrap the yogurt in cheesecloth and hang it overnight on a laundry line.

Note: Leftover batches can be frozen in tightly sealed containers. Just give it a day to thaw to let the bacteria reactivate.

AMISH COOKS ACROSS . . . HONDURAS?

BY KEVIN WILLIAMS

There is no Amish presence in the Americas south of the Rio Grande River. There are some Beachy Amish Mennonite—a more progressive branch of the Anabaptist faith—churches in Central America, and Old Order Mennonites have established colonies in Mexico and Bolivia. But attempts by the Old Order Amish have thus far been unsuccessful. If things had worked out a little differently, this book might well be called *Amish Cooks Across the Americas*.

The Old Order Amish, without a centralized church authority, have a more difficult time establishing the church in other areas. It is left to adventurous families that wish to settle elsewhere to give it a try.

In the 1920s, an Old Order Amish settlement was started in Paradise Valley, Mexico, about 50 miles south of the Rio Grande. The original plan was for ten families to settle on old ranch land. Interest in Mexico was kindled by a desire to escape Ohio's compulsory education laws. In the end, though, only two Amish families settled in Paradise Valley in 1923. And by 1929, even those two families had packed up and headed back for Ohio. Little trace remains today of that ill-fated Amish attempt.

One of the most ambitious attempts to establish an Old Order Church beyond the borders of North America occurred in the 1960s. A group of Amish led by Pathway Publishing founder Joseph Stoll attempted to build a community in Honduras, a long way from his native Canada (see page 22). Numerous challenges surfaced as he tried to start a settlement thousands of miles from home in a land where the language was different and the terrain difficult. The effort is detailed in Stoll's gripping account, *Sunshine and Shadow: Our Seven Years in Honduras* (Pathway Publishing).

Eventually more than a dozen Amish families called Honduras home from 1969 to 1977. An Amish settlement usually doesn't begin to adopt strong connections with local culinary culture until it has existed for fifteen to twenty years. Food traditions are often some of the last to change, because people connect food with comfort and nostalgia.

Pollyanna Yoder was one of the residents of the Honduras settlement. She spent about four and a half years there.

"The way I remember it, most of us stuck to our American-style dishes," Yoder, now living in Ohio, said.

But some adventuresome Amish embraced Honduras's tropical menu. Coffee, corn, and sugarcane were common crops in Honduras in the 1960s. The sugarcane was pressed into *dulce*, chunks of raw brown sugar that were sold as a sweet in the local markets. Roasted ears of Central American corn were often on the supper menus, and raising bees provided a plentiful source for homemade honey. Sorghum molasses didn't seem to do as well in Honduras as it did in the States. The molasses was too bitter to pour onto bread, but it did bake well in cookies. Honey was often used on bread instead.

Many of the Amish had banana patches on their property. Grapefruits were also plentiful in people's yards. Laura Stoll, a member of the settlement, tried making grapefruit pie on several occasions. What follows is one of Pollyanna's recipes, as well as a recipe for corn tortillas that did prove to be a winner among the Canadian transplants.

GRAPEFRUIT PIE
Makes one 9-inch pie

Grapefruits were enjoyed as snacks and the juice was canned, but it took several attempts by residents of the Honduras Amish community to come up with a tasty pie. For the pie shell, you can use a half recipe of the Never-Fail Pastry (page 24) and save the remaining dough for another use.

1 (9-inch) pie shell (see Never-Fail Pastry, page 24)

¾ cup sugar, more or less, depending on your taste and the tartness of the grapefruit

3 tablespoons cornstarch

1¾ cups water

Pinch of salt

1 (3-ounce) box strawberry-flavored gelatin, such as Jell-O

3 or 4 medium-size grapefruits

Whipped cream

Preheat the oven to 350°F. Bake the pie shell until golden brown, about 15 minutes. Cool completely.

Cook the sugar, cornstarch, water, and salt in a medium saucepan over medium heat until clear. Add the gelatin and stir until the mixture slightly thickens. Peel and cut away all pith from the grapefruits, then drain in a strainer and cut into small pieces. Do not use the juice in this recipe. Add the grapefruit pieces to the gelatin mixture. Stir well, pour into the cooled 9-inch pie shell, and refrigerate until set. Top with whipped cream.

CORN TORTILLAS
Makes twelve 6-inch tortillas

Although Dorcas Martin now lives in Aylmer, Ontario, her parents, Sarah and John, lived in Honduras during the 1970s. Dorcas recalls her family greatly enjoying this traditional Honduran dish. "We would add a little lettuce or a little chili sauce to our folded-up tortilla," she said.

2 cups corn flour (masa harina)

½ teaspoon salt

1 to 1¼ cups warm water

Combine the corn flour and salt in a small mixing bowl. Add 1 cup of water, a little at a time, as you continue to mix the ingredients. Knead the dough, adding more water if necessary to keep the dough moist and holding its shape. Let the dough rest for 25 to 30 minutes.

Divide the dough into twelve balls, each the size of a medium egg. Press and pat the balls into a tortilla shape, or use a tortilla press. Place each tortilla on an ungreased hot griddle, and cook until golden brown. When the bubbling stops, turn the tortilla, and brown the other side. Remove from the griddle while the tortilla is pliable. Stack the finished tortillas to keep them moist and warm. Use immediately or allow to cool.

STARTING FROM SCRATCH

Although the Amish made several attempts to establish a community in Texas, only the one in Beeville has endured. Because of the state's distance from other Amish areas, most communities have fizzled after a few years. So what ingredients are necessary for the long-term success and survival of a settlement?

Economic opportunity is one. There needs to be ample opportunity to make a living, either through arable land, home businesses, or even factory work. In the absence of any of those, attracting new residents can be challenging.

Sharing a common ideology *or* acceptance of a wide variety of other opinions can also work. In some cases, new settlements are founded on a very narrow ideology, which can make it difficult to attract new residents and can cause strain on would-be newcomers who don't share that ideology.

Flat Rock, Illinois (see page 55), was founded in 1995 by a group of Amish who wanted to evangelize a bit more than other Old Order Amish. But they also fostered an acceptance of Amish of all stripes. The combination has worked, and that settlement is thriving.

Fredonia, Pennsylvania (see page 26), was founded with a back-to-basics emphasis. For instance, farming would be done entirely by horse-drawn plow. A combination of good soil, temperate climate, and a shared goal of self-sufficiency has helped the church thrive.

Other churches are torn apart by infighting and inconsistent ideology. David Luthy is an Old Order Amish editor at Pathway Publishing (see page 23). He has chronicled the rise and fall of various Amish settlements in his book *Settlements That Failed*. Amish communities have been attempted in almost all states, but many just couldn't overcome the obstacles inherent in beginning a new settlement.

Outside of Cincinnati, the settlement of Woodsdale, Ohio, pays homage to its Amish past. The settlement thrived in the 1800s but ultimately died out because the group couldn't agree on a consistent theology. The stately brick Amish homes still stand.

ETHRIDGE, TENNESSEE

AT A GLANCE

Date established: 1944

Number of church districts: 10

Culinary highlights: molasses, cornbread, pork and beans

The Amish in the settlement of Ethridge, Tennessee, are among the most conservative in the country. It's a Tennessee time warp, where horse-drawn plows ply the fields and electricity is nowhere to be found.

The conservative nature of these folks was on stark display with their total resistance to photographs, even those of a plate of biscuits on a picnic table in the yard without a person in sight. The only way to photograph those biscuits was to take the recipe home, make a batch, and photograph them there.

The town of Ethridge isn't much more than a strip of shops along US 43. There's the "Amish Welcome Center" that offers wagon rides, as well as a gas station, a long-abandoned bus stop, and the Country Mill Restaurant that advertises "even the Amish come here to eat." The Old Order Amish have long been thought of as farming rural outposts in the Midwest and Middle Atlantic states, from Kansas to Delaware, with Ohio and Pennsylvania being their strongholds. The Amish have traditionally—and for a variety of reasons—shied away from the South. But that is slowly changing. Buggies can now be seen in Mississippi, North Carolina, and Arkansas. Spread among the rippling hills in the middle of the Volunteer State is a sprawling Amish settlement made up of Swartzentruber Amish, the most conservative sect (see page 112).

Clothing is fastened with straight pins and buggies do not display the slow-moving vehicle emblem or even gray reflective tape. Swartzentruber Amish have gone to court in many states to preserve their right to keep their buggies black.

Ten church districts make for a large Southern Swartzentruber community. And since the first Amish arrived here in 1944, the settlement's cooking has taken on a definite dash of Dixie. Okra is a staple of gardens, and fields of sorghum are spun into thick, homemade blackstrap molasses. Menus feature hummingbird cake, homemade tea, and hominy.

The Gingerich family just off the main Ethridge artery is typical of the families in the area. Mrs. Gingerich prepares hominy for her family frequently, and she home cans it so that she can enjoy it all year.

"It takes about a quart to feed our family for one meal," Gingerich said.

Tennessee in June can be an oven, but Gingerich seemed unfazed, sitting in her living room on a day drenched with the South's heavy heat and humidity. She's thirty-five years old and has a family of nine children. When winter does decide to make a fleeting visit during January and February, the Gingeriches heat their home with wood. Cooking is done with woodstoves.

Although weddings in more northern climes are traditionally held May through October, here the matrimonial calendar works the other way.

Another Amish woman—we'll call her Esther Miller—lives in a tidy home next to the Gingeriches. Like many of the most conservative Amish, she declined to give her name. Many Amish just view any sort of mainstream media (books, newspapers, TV) with some suspicion, and there's always the fear of appearing "showy." Her tight white *kapp* covers a bun of graying hair. She wears round glasses and offers a ready smile. Using white open-pollinated corn, she goes about preparing hominy and biscuits, while her husband farms their 108 acres.

Miller sells fried pies from her home each Saturday. She's been making the fruit-filled pies for seventeen years, improving upon a recipe a friend gave her, a recipe that she declines to share with anyone.

"But I will tell you that the secret is in the crust," Miller said, standing on her wooden flatboard porch surrounded by thistle sock finch feeders.

"Everyone down here has a lot of success growing okra," she noted. "They just fry it up in cornmeal."

SOUTHERN GAL BISCUITS
Makes 12 biscuits

These are easy biscuits that are best enjoyed sliced in half and drizzled with homemade molasses. Like many Amish recipes the name is lost to history, but the suggestion is that when Amish visited their northern brethren, they found this biscuit to be a different variation. So the baker's biscuits were hung with the name "Southern Gal."

2 cups sifted all-purpose flour

4 teaspoons baking powder

½ teaspoon salt

½ teaspoon cream of tartar

2 tablespoons sugar

½ cup shortening

⅔ cup milk

1 large egg

Preheat the oven to 450°F.

Sift together the flour, baking powder, salt, cream of tartar, and sugar in a large mixing bowl. Add the shortening, and blend until the mixture has the consistency of cornmeal. Slowly pour the milk into the mixture. Add the egg and stir until a stiff dough is formed. Add more flour if needed.

Drop the dough by tablespoons onto a baking sheet. Bake for 10 to 15 minutes, or until the tops begin to turn golden.

CORNBREAD

Serves 12

This is a Southern classic that is enjoyed with soup, spread with butter, or drizzled with homemade molasses. Amish in more northern communities have not traditionally made cornbread.

2 cups cornmeal	1 teaspoon salt
2 cups all-purpose flour	3 large eggs
½ cup sugar	2 cups milk
8 teaspoons baking powder	½ cup melted lard or oil

Preheat the oven to 400°F. Grease a 9 by 13-inch baking pan.

Sift together the cornmeal, flour, sugar, baking powder, and salt in a large mixing bowl. Add the eggs, milk, and melted lard, and stir the mixture until all the ingredients are thoroughly combined. Pour into the prepared pan and bake until the edges are golden brown, 20 to 25 minutes.

HOMEMADE MOLASSES

Many of the Amish homes in the Ethridge area have a small outbuilding similar to the "sugar shacks" in the Conewango Valley of New York (see page 2). But instead of being used to make maple syrup, these buildings are "sorghum sheds," used to make molasses.

"We raise the sorghum, and when it is ready to harvest, it goes through a press and into a tank and then a molasses pan. We make molasses in the fall," said Mrs. Noah Gingerich.

The molasses is then used and enjoyed year-round in cooking, gingerbread, and bread. Often the molasses is simply poured over some homemade biscuits. Enough molasses is put up for use year-round, and, "We sell what we can't use." Many of the Amish farms around Ethridge operate home-based businesses, many of them selling sorghum molasses.

PORK 'N' BEANS
Serves 12

The Amish have heartily adopted this Southern staple. One common Southern variation is to add a couple of tablespoons of homemade sorghum molasses to give it a bit of sweetness.

1 pound dried navy beans or
    Great Northern beans

2 tablespoons salt

8 cups water

1 pound boneless pork,
    cut into very small pieces

SAUCE

1 cup firmly packed brown sugar

½ cup granulated sugar

½ teaspoon black pepper

1 teaspoon dry mustard

1 teaspoon salt

1 quart tomato juice

2 cups water

1½ cups ketchup

¼ cup cornstarch

Remove any debris from the beans, then rinse them and cover them with water in a large bowl. Add the salt and let soak for 8 hours or overnight. Drain and rinse the beans three times, then cover them with the 8 cups water, bring the water to a boil, add the pork, then decrease the heat to low. Simmer until the beans are soft and the pork is cooked through, 45 to 60 minutes. Drain the beans and pork, and set aside.

While the beans are cooking, make the sauce: Place all the sauce ingredients in a large saucepan and bring to a boil over medium-high heat. Decrease the heat to medium-low. Cook the sauce mixture, stirring occasionally, until it is reduced and thickened, about 1 hour.

About 10 minutes before the cooking is finished, preheat the oven to 375°F. Combine the pork mixture with the sauce and pour into a large casserole dish. Bake in the preheated oven, stirring occasionally, until thickened and bubbly, about 40 minutes.

VANILLA ICE CREAM
Makes 1 gallon

This cool classic is a Southern staple in Amish settlements, assuming an ice house is on the premises. Otherwise homemade ice cream has to wait until winter, when Mother Nature supplies the ice. Amish-made ice creams are simpler and don't usually call for overnight freezing. Since this one calls for raw eggs, people with health concerns may want to avoid it, just to be cautious.

6 large eggs

2 cups sugar

½ teaspoon salt

1 tablespoon vanilla extract
  (or other flavoring of your choice)

1 quart heavy cream

1 quart whole milk

Beat the eggs in a large mixing bowl and gradually add the sugar, beating until the mixture is light in color. Add the salt, vanilla, cream, and milk, and mix until thoroughly combined and creamy. Pour into a 1-gallon ice-cream maker and follow the manufacturer's directions. When done, let sit in the freezer for 2 hours before serving.

WHO ARE THE SWARTZENTRUBER AMISH?

The Swartzentrubers are generally considered to be among the most conservative sects of the Old Order Amish. The Swartzentrubers, who are named after an early bishop of the church, split from the mainline Amish church in 1917. The Swartzentrubers wanted to return to the church's less worldly ways. The movement caught on and the Swartzentrubers can now be found in seventeen states.

The Swartzentrubers differentiate themselves from their other Amish brethren by wearing muted, dark clothing. Women's dresses are longer than those in other Amish churches. The Swartzentruber Amish generally don't associate with more liberal Amish churches. They've also resisted perceived government intrusion on their lives more forcefully than other Amish, protesting against the orange safety triangle that many states require on the back of their buggies.

The largest community of Swartzentruber Amish can be found in Wayne County, Ohio, which is where the church began.

PONTOTOC, MISSISSIPPI

AT A GLANCE

Date established: 1996

Number of church districts: 1

Culinary highlights: Muscadines, pecans, sweet potatoes

The Amish had not had a history in the Magnolia State before 1996. But that all changed when a group of Amish from Ethridge, Tennessee, some 150 miles to the northeast on the famed Natchez Trace, came to town.

Pontotoc's Amish community is a daughter settlement of Ethridge, Tennessee. The church community has thrived and has more than twenty-five families and three schools. This area of Mississippi is known for its sweet potato crops, although the Amish themselves don't grow a lot of those to sell. According to Old Order Amish homemaker and Pontotoc resident Dannie Hostetler, the Amish here generally raise sorghum, and others grow produce to sell. Muscadines (a grape variety) and pecans are other local crops that the Amish cultivate and incorporate into their foods.

Nancy Maxey, a non-Amish woman, moved to Pontotoc about the same time as the Amish and quickly befriended many of them, sharing a love of quilting. She described the differences between Pontotoc and Ethridge.

"There are far fewer families and it is not as spread out as Ethridge," she said, explaining that a lot of Amish people left Ethridge because the area had become increasingly touristy. Maxey identified a delicate balance between the Amish, English, and commerce, a balance that can be seen in most Amish settlements: "They need us for the commerce, but they'd rather do it on an individual basis and not by the busload."

Maxey said the Amish have generally been accepted and welcomed by the locals.

"The Amish do come to town and buy seed and do their shopping. Everybody is very respectful. Even the Walmart put a trough out for their horses and gave them their own parking lot for nonmotorized vehicles. The community is very accepting of them," she said.

Some locals were puzzled by some seeming contradictions in Amish culture (see page 106). "They had all the electricity taken out of their homes. But then they use gasoline motors to run their equipment. They don't use hay balers on their property, but then hire non-Amish people who use hay balers," one local woman said.

But Maxey and the Amish, having come to town about the same time, forged a friendship as newcomers.

"Some of my greatest experiences with them have been on Sunday after church, sitting with them, all the family together, sitting there talking in front of the woodstove," she said.

Their homemade peanut brittle is a favorite Amish dish for her to sample. The Amish also make homemade pies, "but they don't use as much sugar as us English people do."

Barn raisings are a relative rarity in established Amish settlements, but in new ones like Pontotoc they are more common. Maxey has attended two.

"It was so awesome to see a community coming together and helping each other build their houses, just like at the movies where they all got together, built it on the ground, and lifted it up," Maxey said. "They start a couple of weeks earlier to make the foundation, but the day of the barn raising, that day they start early, and all the women and the kids come."

During the day, the women usually quilt and prepare meals for the workers. The men would be served separately and first. "It's wonderful seeing twelve to fifteen women around a quilt, quilting it with such little stitches," she said.

Another Pontotoc custom Maxey has observed is for parents to hold a sale after the last child has wedded and left home. "They have a sale to sell the stuff the children don't need anymore."

Of course, in Mississippi, one of the hallmarks of life is the summer heat, but Maxey noted the Amish even have figured out ways to beat that. "They just take it in stride. They build [their houses] so the air blows right through them," she said. And, of course, ice water becomes a treat for people who don't have electric ice makers.

"When I owned a restaurant, they'd come in and get ice water. That was a real treat," Maxey said.

Perhaps the biggest culinary distinction of the Pontotoc Amish is their embrace of the local specialty, muscadines.

"They are native to Pontotoc County, which is known as "land of the hanging grapes; they grow here quite well, we have the ideal climate," Maxey said. Size-wise, muscadines fall someplace between a red grape and a plum. Amish cooks in Pontotoc use them primarily in pies and jellies.

PECAN PIE
Makes one 9-inch pie

Pecan pie is enjoyed by many Amish in the South. Its counterpart in northern settlements, oatmeal pie, is a similar confection, but made with walnuts instead of pecans.

3 tablespoons melted butter

2⅓ cups firmly packed light brown sugar

3 large eggs, beaten

¾ cup light corn syrup

½ teaspoon salt

1 teaspoon vanilla extract

½ cup whole milk

1 cup chopped pecans

1 (9-inch) unbaked pie shell (see
Never-Fail Pastry, page 24)

Preheat the oven to 400°F.

Place the melted butter in a medium saucepan, add the brown sugar, and stir over medium heat until the sugar is dissolved. Slowly add the eggs, stirring constantly, until all the ingredients are thoroughly mixed. Add the corn syrup, salt, and vanilla. Continue stirring the mixture until it comes to a full boil, about 5 minutes. Remove the mixture from the heat. Stir in the milk and pecans until all the ingredients are thoroughly combined.

Pour the filling into the unbaked pie shell and bake for 15 minutes. Decrease the oven temperature to 300°F and bake for another 45 minutes, or until a knife inserted in the center of the pie comes out clean. If the crust edges are getting too brown while baking, cover the edges with foil until the last 5 minutes of baking, at which time the foil should be removed. Let cool completely before serving.

MUSCADINE PIE

Makes one 9-inch pie

Muscadines are commonly seen in farmers' markets across the South. North Carolina has gone so far as to name them its state fruit. Once the Amish moved into the Carolinas, they made this fruit a favorite.

1 quart muscadine grapes, skins removed

1 cup sugar

1½ tablespoons fresh lemon juice

2 tablespoons all-purpose flour

⅛ teaspoon salt

¼ teaspoon ground cinnamon

1 recipe Never-Fail Pastry (page 24)

Preheat the oven to 425°F.

In a small saucepan, cover the grape skins with water and boil until very tender, about 30 minutes. In another saucepan, combine the muscadine pulp and the sugar. Bring the pulp mixture to a near boil over medium heat, then decrease the heat and simmer for 15 minutes. Press the cooked pulp mixture through a sieve to remove the seeds. Drain the water from the cooked hulls and add them to the pulp.

Form a paste in a separate bowl by mixing the lemon juice, flour, and salt. Add the paste to the muscadine pulp and skins, and stir until well combined. Stir in the cinnamon.

Roll out half of the pastry dough on a lightly floured surface until it is large enough to fit into a 9-inch pie pan. Transfer the dough to the pan and gently press it in. Pour the muscadine filling into the crust. Roll out the top crust large enough to cover the filling, transfer it, trim off the excess, and crimp the edges shut. Bake the pie until the crust is golden brown, about 20 minutes.

SORGHUM MOLASSES COOKIES
Makes 3 dozen medium-size cookies

These cookies are infused with the rich taste of locally made sorghum molasses. They are a staple in Amish homes in Pontotoc. The Amish of Pontotoc would not have a refrigerator to chill the cookie dough, but this step has been added to the instructions for better baking.

1 cup shortening

2 cups firmly packed brown sugar

2 cups molasses

2 large eggs

6½ cups all-purpose flour

1 teaspoon salt

4 teaspoons baking soda

2 teaspoons ground ginger

2 teaspoons ground cinnamon

½ teaspoon ground cloves

1 cup buttermilk

½ cup granulated sugar, for rolling the dough

Preheat the oven to 375°F.

In a large mixing bowl, mix the shortening, brown sugar, molasses, and eggs. In a separate bowl, sift together the flour, salt, baking soda, ginger, cinnamon, and cloves. Add the dry mixture alternately with the molasses mixture and the buttermilk. Stir until well blended.

Chill the dough for 1 hour. Remove the dough from the refrigerator and shape into walnut-size balls. Roll them in the sugar and place them about 2 inches apart on a greased cookie sheet. Bake for 10 to 12 minutes, or until set. Transfer to a wire baking rack to cool.

SWEET POTATO SURPRISE CAKE
Serves 10 to 12

This recipe sweetens the sweet potatoes, making it more a dessert than an accompaniment to the main dish, hence the name "surprise cake." If you're expecting supper when preparing this, think dessert instead! Note the coconut in the recipe. Historically coconut has not been part of Amish culinary culture, but over the past fifty years as it's become more readily available in shops, it has become widely used.

1½ cups vegetable oil

2 cups sugar

4 large eggs, separated

¼ cup hot water

2½ cups all-purpose flour

1 tablespoon baking powder

¼ teaspoon salt

1 teaspoon ground cinnamon

1 teaspoon ground nutmeg

1½ cups grated raw sweet potatoes

1 cup chopped walnuts

1 teaspoon vanilla extract

FROSTING

1 (12-ounce) can evaporated milk

1 cup sugar

½ cup (1 stick) butter

3 large egg yolks

1 teaspoon vanilla extract

1⅓ cups shredded coconut

Preheat the oven to 350°F. Grease and flour three 9-inch round cake pans and set aside.

Combine the vegetable oil and sugar in a large mixing bowl and mix well. Add the egg yolks, beating until smooth in consistency. Stir in the hot water, then add the flour, baking powder, salt, cinnamon, and nutmeg. Mix well to form a smooth batter. Stir in the grated sweet potatoes, the nuts, and vanilla until the ingredients are thoroughly mixed. In a separate bowl, beat the egg whites until stiff peaks are formed, and fold the egg whites into the sweet potato mixture.

Pour the batter into the prepared cake pans and bake for 25 to 30 minutes, until the center is cooked through. Let cool completely.

To make the frosting, combine the evaporated milk, sugar, butter, egg yolks, and vanilla in a medium saucepan. Cook over medium heat, stirring constantly, for 12 minutes, or until the mixture thickens. Stir in the coconut. Spread the frosting between the layers of the cooled cake and on the outside of the cake.

CHOUTEAU, OKLAHOMA

AT A GLANCE

Date established: 1910

Number of church districts: 4

Culinary highlights: cornbread, barbecue

Oklahoma is not a state that typically brings to mind a large Amish presence, but it does have an Amish settlement whose roots reach back to almost the turn of the twentieth century. An Amish settlement of four church districts sits just to the west of Chouteau, Oklahoma. The sprawling city of Tulsa is a straight shot 40 miles west.

"I would guess half the men here are farmers, while the others work for carpenter crews and some run small businesses," said Freda Yoder, an Amish resident of the community since 1983, who moved to the area from northern Indiana. "We have a few furniture builders and two little stores."

"Our dress is kind of like it is back in Indiana, but we don't live as fast-paced; it's more laid-back, more slow. We have more farmers here," Yoder said.

The slower pace here mirrors that of Southern life. Greens, baked beans, cornbread, and sweet tea are found on Amish menus here, reflective of the community's Southern surroundings. Despite the church being more than a century old, the community has not

grown substantially over the years. Amish families in the Chouteau area have traditionally been smaller than those found elsewhere.

Freda Yoder is typical of the Amish cooks found in Chouteau. She loves to make big, hearty meals and to bake cookies.

"I like to cook a big meal of meats, potatoes, gravy, vegetables, dinner rolls—cook a meal like mashed potatoes and gravy," Yoder said. She and her husband, Enos, have five children. Enos grew up in Chouteau and met Freda in Indiana. They married and moved back to Oklahoma. Enos enjoys simpler fare for supper.

"My husband would eat mashed potatoes, meat loaf, and sweet corn for every meal if I would make it." Other specialties that Freda fixes are homemade soft pretzels and cheese dipping sauce, and homemade chocolate pie.

Chouteau has not escaped the trend toward Tex-Mex that has found its way into many Amish kitchens across the country. One of Freda Yoder's favorites to fix is homemade cheese enchiladas.

"A lot of people like Mexican food here in our community. So many of them fix it different ways," she said.

Oklahoma is in tornado alley, but the Chouteau settlement has remained untouched. "In the twenty-eight years I have lived here, we have not had a tornado here," Freda Yoder said. But the Oklahoma weather does tend to more extremes than the Amish settlements in Ohio, Indiana, and Pennsylvania. Arctic air can plunge down through the Plains and hit Chouteau with near-zero temperatures a few days a year, and summer can smother the Sooner State to a frying-pan crisp. The summer of 2011, for example, saw fifty days where the temperature exceeded 100 degrees, with the hottest being 116. Because of the warmth, the growing season is longer than in other Amish areas.

"We hardly ever have a white Christmas," Freda Yoder said, although 2010 did feature one. "The first real killing frost sometimes holds off until Thanksgiving, and we start planting in March. I like to have my tomato plants and green beans in by March 30," she said.

One crop that is a little more difficult to grow in Oklahoma is potatoes, but sweet corn is prized. Northeastern Oklahoma is known for its beautiful blooming azaleas each spring. Busloads of tourists will come from Tulsa or Muskogee to eat a meal in an Amish home, then go to a nearby park to see the azaleas.

"They are really pretty," Freda Yoder said, adding that several women in the Chouteau community serve meals in their homes to visitors.

One food that's home canned by some of the Chouteau Amish is homemade barbecue sauce—and you don't find that in many other places.

BUTTERY CORNBREAD
Serves 16

Locally milled cornmeal from the Shawnee Milling Company 100 miles away from Chouteau adds a home-state twist to this Southern favorite. There seems to be a lot of support and use of locally made products, such as the cornmeal and barbecue sauce.

12 tablespoons (1½ sticks) butter

1 cup sugar

3 large eggs, beaten

1⅔ cups milk

1¾ cups all-purpose flour

1 cup cornmeal

4½ teaspoons baking powder

1 teaspoon salt

Preheat the oven to 350°F. Lightly grease a 9 by 13-inch pan and set aside.

Cream the butter and sugar in a medium mixing bowl until light and fluffy. In a small bowl, combine the eggs and milk. In a third (medium) bowl, combine the flour, cornmeal, baking powder, and salt. Add the egg and cornmeal mixtures alternately to the butter mixture, stirring well between additions.

Pour the batter into the prepared pan and bake until a toothpick inserted into the center comes out clean, about 25 minutes.

BARBECUED BEEF SANDWICHES
Makes 8 sandwiches

This is great with roasted potatoes, baked beans, and cold lemonade. Most of the Amish families in Chouteau use home-canned, freshly butchered beef in this recipe. The beef is cut into chunks, pressure-cooked, canned, and stored for later use.

2 pounds chunk meat (see headnote) or leftover roast

1 cup barbecue sauce, or as desired (see Note)

¼ cup firmly packed brown sugar

Salt and black pepper

8 hamburger buns

Combine the meat, sauce, brown sugar, and salt and pepper in a large saucepan. Cook over medium heat until the meat shreds easily and the sauce is bubbling. Serve on hamburger buns.

Note: Your favorite barbecue sauce will work. You could also make your own, using one of the two recipes that follow.

HOMEMADE BARBECUE SAUCE
Makes 18 pints

This homemade barbecue sauce recipe is really popular in the Chouteau community. Amish cooks in Chouteau make this in very large batches so it can be canned, stored, and used throughout the year, but you can reduce and adjust the quantities to fit your needs.

15 cups tomato juice

4 cups chopped onions

¾ cup fresh lemon juice

⅔ cup sugar

2 (5-ounce) bottles Worcestershire sauce

3 cups vinegar

8 cups firmly packed brown sugar

¾ cup prepared mustard

⅓ cup paprika

⅔ cup liquid smoke

⅔ cup salt

1¾ cups cornstarch

Place all the ingredients in a large stockpot and stir to combine. Bring to a boil over medium heat, stirring again, then remove from the heat. Ladle the hot sauce into hot, sterilized, pint-size canning jars. You'll need about eighteen.

Apply the warm, sterilized lids and bands, and place the jars in a boiling water bath for 10 minutes. Once the jars have cooled, check to make sure the lids have sealed properly. If any haven't, refrigerate and use them immediately.

EASY HOMEMADE BARBECUE SAUCE
Makes 3 cups

It seems like every family has its own secret recipe or slightly different concoction for barbecue sauce. This formula is another favorite from Chouteau.

1 cup ketchup

Small dash of Worcestershire sauce

¼ teaspoon soy sauce

½ teaspoon dry mustard

½ cup firmly packed brown sugar

½ cup vinegar

½ teaspoon ground ginger

½ teaspoon chili powder

2 tablespoons chopped onion

½ cup sugar

¼ cup tomato sauce

Place all the ingredients in a large bowl and stir until they are thoroughly combined. Use the sauce fresh in your favorite recipes, or refrigerate for later use.

AMISH STOVETOP BEANS

Serves 4 to 6

This is a Chouteau favorite served warm over fresh cornbread (see page 121). Home hog butchering is a mainstay of the Amish calendar in Oklahoma, so this recipe is made local by the addition of thick slices of fresh bacon.

1 pound dried white navy beans
1 to 2 pounds fresh bacon, cut into pieces
Salt and black pepper

Cook the beans in a large pot according to the package directions.

Fry the bacon in a large skillet until the bacon has partially cooked and released about ¼ cup of grease. Remove the bacon from the pan and drain it on paper towels. Add the grease to the beans and bring to a simmer. Cook for about 45 minutes, adding salt and pepper to taste. Stir in the bacon and serve.

CHOUTEAU BAKED BEANS

Serves 8 to 10

Reflecting Southern tastes, baked beans are popular in Chouteau, too. This recipe is a little simpler than the version offered in Ethridge, Tennessee (see page 111).

4 cups (2 pounds) chopped roast beef
2 teaspoons black pepper
1 onion, chopped
2 cups barbecue sauce (your favorite, or see page 123)
4 (15-ounce) cans pork and beans, drained
1 cup firmly packed brown sugar

Preheat the oven to 350°F. Grease a roasting pan and set aside.

Cook the beef, pepper, and onion together for 15 minutes, or until the onion is soft. Drain off any liquid that accumulates. Mix in the barbecue sauce, pork and beans, and brown sugar. Pour the mixture into the prepared pan.

Bake, uncovered, for 30 minutes. Remove the pan from the oven and stir. Return the pan to the oven and cook for 30 minutes more, or until bubbly.

CHEESY ENCHILADAS
Serves 6 to 8

Freda Yoder said she also makes her own enchilada sauce for this dish. Take any amount of tomato juice and the same amount of tomato sauce, and add a powdered enchilada seasoning, a little brown sugar, and salt to taste. "We like to pour enchilada sauce over the filled tortillas," she said, "then cheese sauce on top of that. Our children like chicken the best with this, but you can use hamburger."

½ cup (1 stick) margarine

¼ cup all-purpose flour

3 cups milk

8 ounces Velveeta cheese, cut into small cubes

2 pounds ground chicken or beef

1 medium-size onion, chopped

12 Flour Tortillas (page 167)

1 cup enchilada sauce

Melt the margarine in a medium saucepan over medium heat. Whisk in the flour until a paste forms, and gradually whisk in the milk, heating until the mixture becomes thickened. Stir in the cheese until it is melted through. Remove the sauce from the heat and set aside.

Preheat the oven to 350°F.

In a large skillet, sauté the chicken with the chopped onion until the meat is no longer pink. Divide the meat among the twelve tortillas, roll up, and place, seam side down, in a 9 by 13-inch baking dish. Pour the enchilada sauce over the top, and the cheese sauce over that. Bake until hot and bubbly, about 30 minutes.

PINECRAFT, FLORIDA

AT A GLANCE

Date established: 1925

Number of church districts: 2

Culinary highlights: tropical cuisine, alligator

Most people think of Disney World and orange juice, not the Amish, when they think of Florida. But Florida does have one thriving Amish settlement, and it's unlike any other.

Tucked away in a relatively quiet corner of sprawling Sarasota is a community known as Pinecraft. Pinecraft serves as a winter respite for Amish "snowbirds" seeking a warm break from the harsh, Midwestern climes. In January and February, Pinecraft is at its peak of activity.

Shuffleboard courts are packed with bearded, suspender-clad men and plainly dressed women. The post office, a withering institution sacked by e-mail in most cities, is a throwback in Pinecraft, where people gather to discuss news of relatives back home. Big Olaf's Creamery serves up a multitude of ice cream flavors and is owned by one of the Mennonite ministers of the church. Troyer's restaurant also does a brisk business, adding a touristy touch to the area.

It's Friday afternoon and an Amish woman in a white prayer cap and solid-colored dress grimaces as she begins pedaling across Beneva Road, finally gaining enough speed to sail across to the other side before the light changes. That may be the height of the hard life for the Amish who winter here. Gone, at least for a while, are the tough mornings of milking, feeding the horses, and collecting eggs from the henhouse.

No one knows exactly how many Amish come to Pinecraft during the winter. The streets, though, reflect their namesakes up north, including Graber, Yoder, and Miller. Trees weighted down with heavy, ripening grapefruit stand in yards. If one wonders how an occasional recipe for grapefruit jam or grapefruit pie ends up in the recipe box of an Amish cook in Wisconsin or Illinois, chances are it originated here.

In addition to becoming a winter haven for the Old Order Amish, Pinecraft has also become a way station of sorts for Anabaptists who might be exploring other orders. Perhaps an Old Order Amish young person thinking of leaving the strict confines of the church will come to Pinecraft for a while to explore. An Anabaptist of any age can come here and feel welcome, and as newcomers and transients are the norm, few questions are asked.

"It is much more relaxed here. The Amish have a chance to socialize with people from all orders," said Todd Emrich, president of the Pinecraft Neighborhood Association.

Emrich said that about five hundred homes make up the Pinecraft area. Since many Amish come for only a few weeks at a time, precise numbers of visitors are difficult to gauge.

Bottom line: Pinecraft is a mishmash of tiny cottages and vacation homes. Where else but Pinecraft can you find a 6,000-square-foot home right next to the settlement's smallest dwelling, a 9 by 12-foot bungalow?

While the atmosphere is relaxed, Amish people still adhere to the main church rules. Three-wheeled bicycles provide the most popular mode of transportation, as buggies aren't practical or permitted on the streets of Sarasota. On a recent Sunday morning, a tiny corner lot was packed with bicycles. Inside the house, an Old Order Amish church service was in full swing. Gentle hymns could be heard riding a gentle balmy breeze.

A bit removed from the bustle of Pinecraft's main activity, tucked away on quiet Honore Avenue, there is even a school, Sunnyside, serving about fifty of the area's Amish-Mennonite children. While surrounding Sarasota continues to grow, Todd Emrich doesn't think it'll ever get out of hand.

"Because of zoning, it would be impossible for this to become a very touristy place, growth is so controlled here," Emrich said.

Even the Amish newspaper, the *Budget*, is available for purchase. As the *Budget* scribe for Pinecraft, Sherry Gore has an unparalleled perch to watch the frequent comings and goings in this Sarasota enclave. This is a place where Amish can come and relax.

"They are all here on vacation, that is the difference," Gore said.

But Pinecraft is a tale of two settlements. From April to September, Pinecraft descends into an annual summer slumber—the streets are empty, the beards and the bonnets are gone, and the ubiquitous bikes are parked.

"It becomes a virtual ghost town, with scorching weather to go along with it. For the few of us that are around, it is a lonely time," Gore said.

But come October, the buses begin to arrive and the people, a trickle at first, begin to descend from the frozen north. The Amish generally arrive by bus, and there are even a few charter lines that cater almost exclusively to the Amish who keep Pinecraft bustling during the winter months.

"It's quite a spectacle to see the buses arrive. There are three different groups who are at the bus stop," Gore said. "There are those who are either boarding the bus or getting off. There are those who are either sending their loved ones off or receiving them. And then there are those who stand back and take it all in. We are always there. It is just as much fun to watch each time. You don't want to miss the bus coming in, no matter how many years you've been watching. It is just as exciting each time."

Gore's winter letters to the *Budget* are filled with writings about who is arriving, departing, and visiting. Buggies are replaced with three-wheeled adult tricycles. Days are often spent on nearby Siesta Key.

"They ride their bikes to the bus stop, chain them . . . you'll see a whole line of them chained up by the bus stop. They'll leave their three-wheelers there, get on the bus, and go to the beach for the day. And then they'll come back burnt as all get out, but they still love it," Gore said. The three-wheelers cost only about three to four dollars a day to rent, or are even cheaper by the week.

Evenings are spent visiting with friends in Pinecraft Park, a place of playgrounds, picnic tables, fishing, and shuffleboard courts. The waterway at Pinecraft has two small manatees, alligators, a boat ramp, and some diehard fishermen and fisherwomen. "There's an Amish grandmother who . . . is sitting on a bucket, fishing each day." Gore laughed. Some of the more adventuresome Amish men take charter boats far out in the Gulf of Mexico for some deep-sea fishing. They hope to catch prized red snapper.

"When you have those fillets, you have it made," Gore said.

Amish foods in Pinecraft are a cross-cultural cauldron, a reflection of the citrus setting and the diverse locales from which people come.

"The Amish do come down here and take advantage of the produce. The farmers' market in town sells pineapples, mangoes, oranges, and avocados. Many of the Amish visitors enjoy fresh avocado slices, Florida avocados," Gore said, noting that strawberries also arrive early and are a favorite. But in addition to sampling the local cuisine, they bring some of their own from their northern settlements.

"Some of them bring that food down. One lady arrived on the bus recently bringing down enough raspberries, ground cherries, corn, and cheese to last her the whole winter here," Gore said.

Here are some recipes shared by Sherry Gore and some of her "plain" friends in Pinecraft:

ORANGE SUPREME PIE

Makes one 9-inch pie

This is a delicious, citrusy pie that has become a Florida favorite among the Amish visitors to Pinecraft.

2 cups water

1 cup granulated sugar

2 tablespoons instant Clear Jel (page 61),
   or 1 tablespoon cornstarch

1 teaspoon orange Kool-Aid

3 oranges, peeled and chopped

4 ounces cream cheese, softened

2 cups powdered sugar

1 (8 ounce) container whipped topping, thawed, plus more for serving

1 (9-inch) prebaked pie shell (see Never-Fail Pastry, page 24)

Bring 1½ cups of the water to a boil in a small saucepan. In a small mixing bowl, combine the granulated sugar, Clear Jel, and Kool-Aid, stir in the remaining ½ cup water, and mix until the ingredients are thoroughly combined. Pour the sugar mixture into the boiling water, stirring as it cooks. Remove the saucepan from the heat when the mixture begins to thicken a bit. Allow the mixture to cool, then stir in the orange pieces.

In a medium bowl, stir together the cream cheese and powdered sugar until creamy. Fold in the whipped topping until the ingredients are thoroughly combined. Spoon the cream cheese mixture into the baked piecrust. Top with the orange filling. Refrigerate until chilled and set, about 1 hour. Top with extra whipped topping, if desired.

SOUTHERN BREEZE PUNCH

Serves 8 to 12

This is a thirst-quenching concoction shared with us by Esther Schlabach. It's very refreshing and attractive, and not too sweet.

¼ cup blue raspberry Kool-Aid powder

1 cup sugar

7 cups water

1 (46-ounce) can pineapple juice

1 (6-ounce) can frozen lemonade concentrate

2 liters ginger ale

In a very large bowl or container, combine all the ingredients and stir to dissolve and evenly distribute them. To serve, fill a glass with ice cubes, then pour the mixture over the ice to fill the glass. Stir the mixture briskly and allow a few minutes for the cubes to thaw into the punch.

THE PIONEER BUS LINE

One of Pinecraft's lifelines is the Pioneer bus. Many Amish couldn't afford to hire drivers to take them on the long journey from their Midwestern homes to Sarasota. The Pioneer bus provides an affordable option and helps the Pinecraft economy by supplying a steady stream of visitors during the winter months.

The company started in 1982 to serve a growing market for "Amish snowbirds" seeking a respite from the tough Midwestern winters. Since its origins serving the Amish, Pioneer has grown into a diversified bus company serving colleges and charter groups.

"The Florida line is now only about 10 to 15 percent of our business, but it comes at a good time during the winter when we are slow with our other stuff," said Wendyl Swartzentruber, whose father started the Ohio-based company. Swartzentruber is himself several generations removed from the Amish.

"The busiest time for our Florida run, which is less than twenty-four hours from Indiana, is February and March," Swartzentruber said. Most bus runs from northern Indiana or Ohio to Florida take 22 hours, much of it overnight. Of course, variables such as traffic and weather can cause the time to fluctuate.

"We started out with a lot of Amish, but we are sort of growing in non-Amish people. A lot of them are elderly . . . people . . . going down for a little vacation time."

FLORIDA AVOCADO–EGG SCRAMBLE
Serves 4 to 6

Sherry Gore said that although avocados are not a food that most Amish eat in their Midwestern homes, that's not so in Florida, where avocados are so commonplace that many people eat them sliced or scrambled in with some eggs.

1 Florida avocado, halved lengthwise,
    skin and pit discarded, and cut into medium dice
Salt
8 large eggs
½ cup sour cream
1 teaspoon black pepper
1 tablespoon butter

Sprinkle the diced avocado with salt and set aside.

In a medium mixing bowl, beat the eggs with the sour cream until thick and creamy; season with additional salt and the pepper. Melt the butter in a medium skillet over medium-low heat. Add the egg mixture and cook, stirring occasionally. When almost set, gently fold in the avocado. Serve immediately.

FRUITY FLORIDA COLESLAW
Serves 8 to 10

Featuring some of Florida's best fruits, this is a popular dish for gatherings. Cortland apples go well in this salad, because their flesh is slow to brown after cutting.

1 head cabbage, shredded

2 Florida oranges (or equivalent amount of canned mandarin oranges)

2 Cortland apples, peeled and chopped

1 cup red seedless grapes

1 (16-ounce) can pineapple chunks, drained

½ cup chopped walnuts

¼ cup sweetened flaked coconut

Pinch of salt

½ cup mayonnaise

¾ cup whipped topping, thawed

1 tablespoon sugar

1 tablespoon fresh lemon juice

Place the cabbage, oranges, apples, grapes, pineapple, walnuts, and coconut in a large bowl and toss to combine. Mix the salt, mayonnaise, whipped topping, sugar, and lemon juice in a small bowl. Pour the dressing over the cabbage mixture, mix well, and serve in your prettiest glass bowl.

FLORIDA VEGETABLE MEDLEY
Serves 4 to 6

This is another of Sherry Gore's recipes featuring fresh Florida produce.

6 to 8 small Florida squash, sliced

6 ripe Florida tomatoes, cut into wedges

6 Florida onions (the sweetest variety you can find), sliced

Salt and lemon pepper

½ cup water

Grated sharp Cheddar cheese, for garnish

Place a layer of sliced squash in a large skillet, then add a layer of tomato wedges and a layer of sliced onions. Continue layering until all the vegetables are used. Sprinkle with salt and lemon pepper as desired. Add the water and steam over medium heat for 12 to 15 minutes, until the vegetables are tender. Serve in a pretty dish with the cheese sprinkled on top.

GRILLED LIME FISH FILLETS
Serves 4 to 6

Lime and other citrus fruits are not common in Amish kitchens in the North. Traditionally, oranges might be something reserved for special occasions. But in Pinecraft, citrus grows in the tiny yards and finds its way into many recipes—such as this one. This recipe can be used with any fresh-caught fish. Snapper is a favorite Gulf of Mexico catch.

2 pounds frozen fish fillets, thawed
About 2 tablespoons canola oil
Paprika
½ cup (1 stick) butter, melted
¼ cup fresh lime juice
Salt and black pepper
Lime wedges, for garnish
Cooked white or wild rice, for serving

Brush the fish fillets with the oil and sprinkle with the paprika. Combine the melted butter and lime juice and set aside.

Place the fish on a well-oiled grill, 3 to 4 inches from medium-hot coals. Cook for 5 to 7 minutes on each side, until the fish flakes easily with a fork, basting frequently with the lime juice mixture. Just before serving, sprinkle with salt and pepper. Garnish with fresh lime wedges, and serve with rice.

Variation: Before placing the fish on the grill, place lime slices on one side of the fish, and wrap the fish and lime slices with a strip of uncooked bacon. Secure the bacon with toothpicks, then grill as directed.

FLORIDA ORANGE RICE
Serves 5

This recipe combines citrus and rice to create something that tastes creamy and citrusy. This is another flavorful recipe that is something different from what might be enjoyed in a traditional Midwestern Amish community.

2 cups cooked white rice

2 tablespoons sugar

1½ oranges, cut into pieces

1 cup prepared Dream Whip

Place all the ingredients in a medium mixing bowl and stir until thoroughly combined. Refrigerate until chilled, at least 1 hour, before serving.

FRIED ALLIGATOR NUGGETS
Serves 4 to 6

Alligator meat is fairly common in Florida. Alligator has its own unique flavor that is easily enhanced with the same seasonings and sauces you would use for pork or chicken. You could also use your own favorite dipping sauces. Horseradish, barbecue sauce, honey-mustard, hot pepper, and cocktail sauce are a few other favorites. Alligator meat has a light, fine-grained texture, not unlike some hearty fish fillets.

1 pound alligator meat, cut into
    1-inch chunks or strips

1 cup all-purpose flour, seasoned
    with salt and black pepper

Vegetable oil, for frying

Lime wedges, for serving

Tartar sauce, for serving

Dredge the meat pieces with the seasoned flour. Heat the vegetable oil (about 1-inch deep) in a medium skillet. Add the meat and fry for 2 to 3 minutes, until the pieces float to the top. Drain on paper towels. Serve hot with lime wedges and tartar sauce.

OUR FLORIDA ADVENTURE

BY LOVINA EICHER

I never thought I would get to see the ocean or get to visit the Pinecraft Amish settlement. But Joe and I and our family made a trip to Florida. While we were there, we toured the inside of the church building, which was really interesting to see. It is different to see an Amish church service being held with no buggies in the yard. Instead, they all have bikes or they walk.

A few of our children asked where all the horse and buggies were, and we had to explain to them that the Amish here didn't bring their horse and buggies with them.

It also seems different to see Amish people living in town with no barns or animals, which is typical in Amish communities up north. I think this is a very nice place for the older Amish to stay during the cold winters. Most families with children, like ours, prefer to stay and brave out the snowy cold winters in the North. But I suppose my thoughts on that could change as I get older.

When you haven't seen the ocean, you can only imagine how it looks. But seeing is believing. When looking at it, one can only marvel at the scenic creation God made. It was so peaceful to sit by the ocean and just watch the waves. Having the ocean so close by is another privilege for the Amish in Pinecraft. For the children, seeing the ocean was definitely their favorite part of the trip. The children enjoyed collecting seashells, and they loved seeing the dolphins, too. They all said that they are ready to go again. Benjamin said he "wishes he could see the ocean every day."

We enjoyed a lot of time at the beach. The children spent as much time as they could in the water, and by the end of the week they were all playing in the ocean and braving the waves.

Kevin also took us to Myakka River State Park, where we walked the "canopy walk," a swinging walkway that goes through the treetops, and climbed the 76-foot tower that overlooked the surrounding swamps. We also took an airboat ride and got to see the alligators. Joe ordered the "gator stew" for lunch. He said it was good, but I passed on that.

Another highlight was taking a boat tour out on the ocean and getting to see dolphins. We even got to see one jump up all the way out of the water.

On July 4, we saw a fireworks display from the beach.

Loretta had her eleventh birthday on July 1, while we were traveling. Kevin, my editor, and his wife Rachel presented her with a hamburger-shaped cake that said, "Happy Birthday, Loretta."

One funny memory: Soon after we entered Florida, son Kevin, five, saw a small pond. He yelled out, "I see the ocean!" It gave us all a laugh.

Reading, writing, playing games, singing, all took place on this long journey. We also kept track of how many license plates we saw from different states. Our count was forty.

Citrus trees grow in abundance in the yards of Pinecraft—grapefruits, limes, and oranges. That was something different to see.

UNION GROVE, NORTH CAROLINA

AT A GLANCE

Date established: 1995

Number of church districts: 1

Culinary highlights: blackberries, cereal

North Carolina has never hosted a large Amish population. As of 2011, North Carolina was home to one settlement outside of Union Grove, in the western part of the state. With a temperate climate, arable soil, and large swaths of rural land, the Tarheel State may well be poised for speedy growth in the future. The Union Grove Amish are horse-and-buggy people, and their population is slowly climbing.

Deanna Gaither owns the Kountry Korner restaurant in the heart of Union Grove's Amish settlement. She says the area Amish are some of her best customers. Ironically, whereas a lot of non-Amish come in for a break from the fast-food restaurant wasteland, the Amish customers generally order the fast-food type items from the menu. The young Amish boys love the "rodeo burger" and cheese sticks.

Gaither is an admirer of the Amish in her community, calling them a steady and polite presence.

"I like that when they bring young children into the restaurant, they are always well behaved. And I mean always—unlike other children who are running around, crying, begging, not eating their food yet wanting ice cream. Unlike other parents who, if I've heard it once, I've heard it a million times, say, "Now I told you . . ." Yet the children still get what they want. The Amish children ask once and if they are told no, that is the end of the conversation," Gaither recalled.

Fresh blackberries are a summer staple in Union Grove. They grow well in the rambling, fertile hills of the North Carolina Piedmont. Some Amish families sell the blackberries during the summer. Gaither bought some and baked them into cobblers to sell at her restaurant.

VIOLA'S HOMEMADE CEREAL
Serves 6 to 8

Uriel and Viola Miller were one of the first Amish families in Union Grove. Church members always enjoyed Viola's delicious cereal, which is a lot like Grape-Nuts. After cooling, place the cereal in large bags overnight before crumbling. This cereal is great served in a bowl with milk or just for snacking plain. Like most Amish cooks, Viola makes this in a large batch and stores it in tightly sealed containers, where it will keep fresh for weeks. We halved her recipe for home cooks.

4 pounds whole wheat flour

1¼ pounds brown sugar

1½ teaspoons salt

5 cups buttermilk

2½ teaspoons baking soda

1 tablespoon imitation maple flavoring

1½ teaspoons vanilla extract

¾ cup (1½ sticks) butter, melted

Preheat the oven to 350°F.

Mix the whole wheat flour, brown sugar, and salt in a very large bowl or container until the ingredients are thoroughly combined. In a large mixing bowl, combine the buttermilk and baking soda until smooth. Add the buttermilk mixture to the flour mixture, and stir until the flour mixture is evenly coated. Add the maple flavoring, vanilla, and butter, and stir to evenly incorporate. Spread the mixture evenly on baking sheets.

Bake until nicely browned, about 2 hours. Let cool completely, then crumble into fine pieces and toast in a warm (250°F) oven.

HOMEMADE SALAD DRESSING
Serves 8 to 10

This is a creamy spread that can be used on sandwiches much as you would use Miracle Whip. With a hint of honey, maple, and garlic, a variety of tastes can be enjoyed in a single spread.

1¾ cups water

½ cup vinegar

⅔ cup all-purpose flour

1 large egg, beaten

¾ cup (1½ sticks) butter, softened

2 tablespoons honey

2 tablespoons pure maple syrup

2 teaspoons salt

1 teaspoon fresh lemon juice

1 teaspoon dry mustard

½ teaspoon garlic powder

1 teaspoon paprika (optional)

2 teaspoons dried basil (optional)

Cook the water, vinegar, and flour in a small saucepan over medium heat until thickened, stirring constantly with a whisk. In a large bowl, thoroughly combine the egg, butter, honey, maple syrup, salt, lemon juice, dry mustard, garlic powder, paprika, and basil. Add the flour mixture. Pour everything into a blender, and process until thick and creamy. Pour the dressing into glass jars and refrigerate until ready to use.

HOMEMADE BLACKBERRY CAKE
Serves 10 to 12

This is a favorite recipe in Amish settlements across Virginia and North Carolina, where wild blackberries are plentiful. This is a very moist cake that tastes great frosted. You'll want to have the icing cooked and ready to put on the cake as soon as it is done, while both are still warm.

CAKE

2 cups granulated sugar

4 cups all-purpose flour

½ cup (1 stick) butter, softened

2 cups blackberry jam

1 cup chopped black walnuts

2 teaspoons ground cinnamon

2 teaspoons ground cloves

2 teaspoons ground nutmeg

2 teaspoons ground allspice

2 teaspoons baking soda, dissolved
     in 1 cup buttermilk

6 large eggs

ICING

2 cups granulated sugar

1 cup milk

½ cup (1 stick) butter

Preheat the oven to 300°F. Lightly grease a 9 by 13-inch baking pan and set aside.

Make the cake: Thoroughly mix all of the ingredients in a large mixing bowl until smooth and lump-free. Pour into the prepared pan and bake for 1 hour, or until the cake is firm in the center and a toothpick comes out clean.

Make the icing: During the final 20 minutes of baking, place all the ingredients in a small saucepan over medium heat. Cook, stirring often, until thick. Keep warm until ready to use.

Remove the cake from the oven and pour the icing over it while both are still hot. Let cool completely before serving.

THE AMISH COOK'S
SOUTHERN OBSERVATIONS

I think it would be too hot to live in South Texas or Mississippi! We're used to the seasons in Michigan.

Some of the foods in the Southern chapter are ones I am familiar with, such as cornbread and sweet potatoes. Some of these dishes I have not tried before, such as okra, so it was interesting to read about those recipes. Okra is not something that we grow around here. The hot peppers, though, are gaining in popularity. My family had never used, grown, or eaten hot peppers until Joe's family had us try them after we started dating. At first I didn't care for them, but I remember my mother really liked them. I eat them now, but I like to use serrano peppers when I can them. They aren't quite as hot and stay crispier in the jars. I will, however, use jalapeños in salsa or homemade vegetable juice. We also like to make jalapeño poppers on the grill with them.

CROFTON, KENTUCKY

AT A GLANCE

Date established: 1972

Number of church districts: 2

Culinary highlights: Southern

When the first horse and buggies began showing up on the streets of Crofton, Kentucky, in 1972, locals viewed them with some suspicion, and even resentment.

"They'd come in and buy up the biggest farms, the best farms, and then divided them up among their children . . . so there were some hard feelings among farmers at first," said Karen Dulin, who moved to Crofton three years before the Amish arrived. But over time the Amish have become a welcome part of the landscape of rolling tobacco fields and burley barns.

"They are just supernice people. If someone loses a house or something . . . they are always there to help," Dulin said.

She also pointed to the wide variety of Amish-owned businesses that have boosted the local economy. The Crofton community is home to a variety of Amish businesses, including sawmills, pallets, and milling. The Amish serve meals once a month from an activity building that their church owns.

"The meals are delicious—all kinds of meatloaf, barbecued chicken, pork chops, vegetables, cakes, and pies, the menu changes from month to month. A bit of a Southern flair has shown itself on the menu, which often includes sweet tea, and beans and cornbread.

"The meals remind me of some of the ones that Lovina writes about all of the time, all the different kinds of stuff that she puts out," said Dulin, who is a longtime reader of "The Amish Cook" column.

Kentucky experienced rapid growth in its Amish population during the mid-1990s. Many Amish arrived from Lancaster County, Pennsylvania, where lack of land and suburban sprawl were making it increasingly difficult on the Amish. At the time, sociologists referred to the move to western Kentucky as the biggest mass migration of Amish since they began arriving in the United States.

For most of the state's history, the Amish population in Kentucky was confined to pockets in the rural southwest, especially near Mayfield and Christian County. But the 1990s saw their population grow tremendously, and horse-and-buggy populations can now be found in the northeast part of the state, near Vanceburg and Mays Lick.

Amish cooks in Kentucky reflect the state's straddling between North, South, and Midwest. Sweet potatoes and okra are found in some Amish settlements in some parts of the state, while more traditional cinnamon rolls and shoofly pie are found elsewhere.

KENTUCKY DRESSING

Serves 4 to 6

This is a delicious homemade salad dressing that utilizes easy-to-find ingredients in this rural Kentucky community.

2 cups salad dressing, such as Miracle Whip

⅓ cup vegetable oil

⅓ cup ketchup

¾ cup sugar

¼ teaspoon garlic salt or onion salt

¼ teaspoon paprika

1 tablespoon vinegar

1 teaspoon prepared mustard

1 teaspoon Worcestershire sauce

Combine all the ingredients in a large mixing bowl. Mix with a wire whisk until the dressing is smooth and glossy. Serve the dressing on lettuce salads, or use it to dip fresh vegetables.

SWEET POTATO PUDDING

Serves 4 to 6

Sweet potatoes are common in Southern Amish settlements, but not so much in more traditional Midwestern ones. This is a favorite recipe in Kentucky Amish communities, but is more often reserved for dessert because it is so sweet.

2 cups cooked, mashed sweet potatoes

3 tablespoons sugar

2 large eggs, well beaten

2 tablespoons butter, melted

1 teaspoon salt

1 cup milk

½ cup mini marshmallows or marshmallow crème

Preheat the oven to 350°F.

In a large mixing bowl, combine the sweet potatoes, sugar, eggs, butter, salt, and milk until thoroughly blended. Add the marshmallows and blend well.

Pour the mixture into a buttered 2-quart casserole. Bake for 45 minutes, or until the marshmallows are melted and golden.

SOUTHERN EXPERIMENT: ELMO STOLL AND THE CHRISTIAN COMMUNITIES

While there is no singular leader of the church, some Amish have risen to prominence over the years. One such man was Elmo Stoll, whose brother was one of the founders of Pathway Publishing in Aylmer, Ontario. Elmo Stoll was part restless soul, part visionary. From his perch as editor of the Amish magazine *Family Life*, he spent years writing columns and essays that expounded the virtues of plain living. He envisioned a church that was more accessible and ministerial.

"He was idealistic, perhaps not realistic, but definitely idealistic," said Elizabeth Stoll of her late husband.

The Amish Church generally doesn't keep outsiders from joining; however, the use of the German language makes it difficult for people to join.

"His vision was to have a plain and English-speaking church for Seekers, people who wanted to join. It was a real hurdle for people to learn the German language, although we soon realized language was not the only problem," Stoll said. Elmo was also very intrigued by the Hutterites and their adoption of communal living. Ultimately Elmo Stoll tried to create a blend of Amish and Hutterite. He tried to incorporate the plainness of the Amish with the communality of the Hutterites to make a single church.

"He was very intrigued by communal living; he thought there should be more equality in a community. Some shouldn't have money while others are struggling," Stoll said. She explained, though, that while that sounds like a good idea, it didn't necessarily pan out in practice.

At its height, several states had Christian communities. Members used horse and buggies and lived in close proximity. Some families shared homes for a while, but the communal aspect never really caught on. There were some shared gardens for a time, "but as time went on, we each had our separate things to take care of," Stoll recalled.

But one aspect did catch on: the communal meal after church.

"My husband wanted to keep the tradition of eating together after church. It binds people together. . . . You don't want the ones who feel a little left out going home," she said. The after-church meal was similar to an ordinary Amish church meal, with egg salad, pickles, bread, occasionally peanut butter spread (or "church spread," as it is often called), tomatoes, melons, hot tea, garden mint tea, and iced tea being served. And sometimes the church community would get together for Sunday suppers, which consisted of carry-in foods, usually a hot dish and some kind of salad. And there might be dessert of cake, cookies, and pudding.

At one time there were several such communities across the South, in Arkansas, Tennessee, and Kentucky. Over time, though, most of the settlements disbanded. Today, one fully intact Christian community remains a testament to Elmo Stoll's vision. That settlement is outside Caneyville, Kentucky.

AMISH COOKS ACROSS THE
WEST

For most of Amish history in the United States, the American West was seen as some distant backwater, unsuitable for settlement. But as Amish dependence on farming in the Midwest and East diminished, many Amish have looked westward as a way to escape congestion, high land prices, and busloads of camera-toting tourists.

Montana, with a history of conservation and a live-and-let-live environment, began to seem appealing to the Amish. Until the 1970s, there were only sporadic attempts by the Amish to settle west of the Rockies, and most of those attempts proved unsuccessful. The Amish began settling in Montana as early as 1903, when a group of families arrived from Ohio and put down roots in Dawson County, near the North Dakota border. That community only lasted a few years. But in 1974, a more determined group of Amish decided to head for Rexford, Montana, where there had been a history of conservative Mennonite churches. The Rexford settlement has lasted and has since become a jumping-off point that has led to the start of other Amish settlements.

One of the most ambitious attempts at Western settlement was made in Horsefly, British Columbia. The Amish today in Montana still sometimes talk wistfully about what might have been when referring to Horsefly. In 1969, several Ohio and Indiana Amish families moved to Horsefly, British Columbia, to establish a settlement and work at lumbering. Their farming skills weren't suited to the new environment, and they were so far from other Amish settlements that life there proved to be too difficult, so the settlement only lasted about three years. Today, no trace of the Amish presence in Horsefly remains. A more recent attempt to begin an Amish settlement out West began when several families moved to the Moses Lake, Washington, community. That church also died out due to its isolation.

Although some settlements have failed, others, chiefly in Montana and Colorado, now seem to have lasting Amish settlements, and their success will likely help the success of future Western settlements as the open West continues to become increasingly attractive to the Amish. Even Alaska has been eyed by the Amish as a place to settle, and a couple of conservative Mennonite churches have been established there. As of 2012, Wyoming and Idaho now have their first Amish settlements, offering additional evidence of the church's expansion in the open West. Maybe someday we'll have Amish recipes from Alaska, but in the meantime, we'll pay a visit to cooks in Montana and Colorado.

REXFORD, MONTANA

AT A GLANCE

Date established: 1974

Church districts: 1

Culinary highlights: wild game, huckleberries

Rexford, Montana, has long captivated the Amish imagination. Week after week, entries in the *Budget* (see page 127) provide the Amish out East with a window into a Western world of wild huckleberries, lumbering grizzlies, and mountain creeks packed with trout. It's such a remote corner of Montana, but it has also served as the Amish talisman to restless Western exploration, a beacon of adventure.

Amish, especially young outdoors-loving men, find the opportunities of Rexford appealing. To understand the Amish in Rexford, you have to understand the geography and history first. Start with the geography. Lake Koocanusa is only a mile wide at its widest, but it's a very long lake, stretching more than 90 miles from south to north in Montana's far northwest corner. The lake was created in 1975 by the damming of the Kootenai River outside Libby, just one year after the first Amish moved to Rexford. The lake serves as a giant "wall," dividing the far rural northwest Montana from the rest. A lone bridge connects the east and west sides of Lake Koocanusa, providing the Amish—and anyone else—with a span to travel.

The closest airport to fly into without paying an extremely high fare is Spokane, Washington, about four hours of driving away. That may sound extreme to some, but not to one Amish woman, who said, dismissively, "Four hours isn't a long way. Everything out here is that far away."

Besides the stark majesty of the towering Whitefish Mountains and the unspoiled deep blue beauty of Lake Koocanusa, the area has one striking feature that can be seen immediately: FOR SALE signs. Lots of them. Turns out, these numerous empty houses were not all Amish-owned, nor are they casualties of the Great Recession.

"Oh, it's pretty much always that way around here. People move out here thinking that they'll love the mountains and wilderness, but they often get discouraged at the isolation and move back. It takes a different kind of person to be able to live here year in and year out," said Noah Hostetler, an Amish resident of the Rexford settlement.

While the Amish have for years called the settlement "Rexford," that's a little misleading. It's more than 15 miles on

winding mountain road from the Amish settlement to the tiny "town" of Rexford, which consists of nothing more than an RV park, saloon, general store, and boat launch. Since Rexford is the closest post office, "Rexford" is the mailing address, but local Amish more accurately refer to their community as "West Kootenai," which describes their area.

Libby, 50 miles to the south, has an Amtrak station that serves as a lifeline to the rest of the United States. It's a 2-day train trip to visit family out East. One family in Rexford has a son who lives in Pinecraft, Florida (see page 126), and a train journey there takes 4 days. The Rexford Amish, however, are one of the few groups that will make a concession to speed, if needed.

"We will travel by air if it's an emergency," said Hostetler, a minister in the Rexford church.

A favorite activity of many of the church families is an annual camping trek into the nearby Whitefish Mountains. They'll spend days out in nature, harvesting huckleberries, dodging grizzlies, cooking over a campfire, and just generally enjoying the peace and fellowship.

As for its relatively short history: Although the Amish population of Rexford has ebbed and flowed over the years, it has been a tenacious, scrappy settlement. It has reached a high of close to twenty-five families at various points in its history and fallen to fewer than ten. In 2011, the settlement was hanging on with nine families, but new arrivals were apparently on the way. And the number of young people in the community—often a barometer of the future—seemed to be on the upswing.

"There are about sixteen children in the school now, which is the highest it has been in a while," said one Amish woman.

An auction is held on the second Saturday of each June to raise funds for Mountain View Parochial School, where the Amish scholars (as the Amish refer to students) attend. The West Kootenai Amish Auction includes quilts, crafts, gazebos, log cabins, and baked goods. One of the biggest draws to the event, however, might be the food. The Amish women spend days preparing a lunch of barbecued chicken, side dishes, homemade ice cream, and pie—plenty of pie. Usually about two hundred pies are prepared for the event and sold by the slice. More than one thousand people usually show at the auction, no small feat for such a rural outpost. This has become a signature event in the area, attracting hordes of locals to meet and mingle with the Amish community.

Horse-drawn buggies are used in the Rexford community, but in a very limited way. The community is so closely clustered that there's not a lot of need for them, except maybe to visit someone a mile or two away. A lot of the travel in the settlement is done by bicycle. Those who live higher up in the foothills and who don't want to pedal up the steep grades will often leave their bicycle at the bottom of the hill, so they can come down on foot, jump on their bike, and be on their way. As far as taking the buggy to a nearby store in town, there simply aren't any stores to go to. A buggy ride into Rexford would be an all-day event, so it isn't done. This isolation forces a greater self-sufficiency among the Amish in Rexford.

Most of the Amish men in the settlement work at Montana Woodworks, which produces handmade beds, bookcases, dressers, sofas, and all sorts of other home furnishings, relying on the value of legendary Amish craftsmanship. The business is a hive of bustling and buzzing activity in an otherwise quiet valley.

Wild game is popular in Rexford, with elk and moose meat being the game of choice. Some also eat bear and then use the fat for various household purposes.

"Atlee just shot a bear last week. So I am cooking out the fat to make grease, which I'll use to waterproof his shoes. And bear lard in cooking and baking [is] just like you would use pig lard," said Doris Yoder. She and her husband, Atlee, an avid outdoorsman, run a greenhouse on their property.

"The taste of bear meat depends on what the bear has been feeding on. If it's berries, the meat is really good; if it's other game, the taste isn't so good," she said. Problem is, you don't really know until you taste the meat.

Huckleberries are popular in Rexford and find their way into pies, cobblers, and jams. The berries grow in the wild at elevations of more than 6,000 feet. Attempts by the Amish and others to cultivate the berries at lower altitudes have not been successful.

"People have tried to bring them down and grow them, but it just hasn't worked," said Katherine Hostetler, Noah's wife.

Amish weddings in Rexford feature a menu that is at once traditional Amish and Old West. Katherine Hostetler said the usual peanut butter spread, pickles, and red beets are on the menu. But there are also cold meat sandwiches of the wild game variety: elk and deer bologna, for instance.

"We get enough to last us a year," Katherine said of the wild game harvests.

The meat recipes in this chapter are home processed and call for very large amounts. The reason for that is cultural and practical. If someone comes home having bagged a bear or an elk in a hunt, the Amish won't just can a couple of pounds of meat; they'll use every last ounce of usable meat and store it for use over the long winter. Home cooks can decrease the recipe quantities if trying these at home, using lesser amounts of meat. Here are some recipes common in the settlement.

ELK BOLOGNA

Makes about 30 pounds

Elk is a popular haul among Amish hunters, and plentiful in Montana. Amish cooks report that it has a less gamey taste than venison. The meat in this recipe takes several days to cure, and it makes a large batch to freeze for later.

25 pounds ground elk meat

8 ounces Morton's Tender Quick meat cure

¾ cup firmly packed brown sugar

½ cup salt

½ teaspoon saltpeter

4 teaspoons black pepper

4 teaspoons garlic salt

2 tablespoons liquid smoke

2 quarts water

Mix the ground elk meat in a very large bowl with the Tender Quick, brown sugar, salt, saltpeter, black pepper, garlic salt, and liquid smoke. Refrigerate the mixture for 4 days to allow to cure. After the allotted time, process the meat mixture through a meat grinder. Mix the water into the ground meat mixture and combine thoroughly.

Place the meat mixture in loaf pans, and bake at 175°F for 10 hours. At that point, the meat may be sliced and frozen. Instead of baking, you may also can the meat in sterilized canning jars at 10 pounds of pressure for 1 hour, following your pressure cooker manufacturer's instructions.

VENISON OR ELK SUMMER SAUSAGE
Makes 30 pounds

This is a wonderful recipe that makes a very tender sausage. It makes a great snack with crackers or cheese or to give to someone as a gift. Elk meat is a favorite around here, but deer are often easier to come by, so this recipe can be used in either. Most think elk meat is more flavorful.

30 pounds ground deer or elk meat

2 cups Morton's Tender Quick meat cure

2 cups firmly packed brown sugar

2 tablespoons ground coriander

5 tablespoons onion salt

3½ teaspoons garlic powder

1 teaspoon ground nutmeg

1 tablespoon black pepper

5 teaspoons liquid smoke

2 tablespoons seasoning salt

3 tablespoons Worcestershire sauce

15 cups water

In a very large bowl or container, combine all the ingredients and mix thoroughly. Refrigerate the mixture for 24 hours to allow time to cure.

Preheat the oven to 350°F. Form the meat mixture into 2 by 8-inch logs. Wrap each with aluminum foil, shiny side facing the meat. Place the sausages on rimmed baking sheets and bake for 1½ hours. Allow the sausages to cool, then remove the aluminum foil and drain off the grease. Wrap the sausages in plastic wrap, and refrigerate or freeze until ready to use.

Set out the meat to thaw the night before you're ready to use it. Freezing for storage allows the sausage to keep for a year or longer if tightly sealed.

HUCKLEBERRY PANCAKES
Makes about 2 dozen pancakes

These pancakes are favorites around the breakfast campfire during the annual outings that many Amish families make into the mountains. This pancake recipe uses cornmeal, which gives great balance to the sweet huckleberries.

1½ cups milk

2 eggs, beaten

¼ cup vegetable oil

2 cups all-purpose flour

½ cup cornmeal

1 tablespoon sugar

½ teaspoon salt

4 teaspoons baking powder

1 cup huckleberries

Place the milk, eggs, and vegetable oil in a large mixing bowl, and whisk them until they are thoroughly combined. Add the flour, cornmeal, sugar, salt, and baking powder, and stir until all the ingredients are thoroughly combined. Gently fold the huckleberries into the batter. Drop the batter by quarter-cupfuls onto a hot, greased griddle. Cook the pancakes on the first side until the edges are set and bubbles break the surface, about 1 minute. Flip the pancakes and continue cooking until golden brown and cooked through.

HUCKLEBERRY PIE FILLING
Makes filling for 1 pie

Huckleberries are a favorite among Montana's resident population of grizzly bears, so would-be berry pickers must always be on the alert for these prowling creatures. The grizzly is a protected species, so these bears can't be hunted.

3 cups huckleberries

2 cups water

2 tablespoons Perma-Flo thickener, or 3 tablespoons cornstarch

¾ cup sugar

Salt

Place 1 cup of the huckleberries in a medium saucepan and gently mash with the back of a spoon. Add 1 cup of the water and cook over medium heat for 10 minutes. Meanwhile, in a medium bowl, mix together the Perma-Flo thickener, sugar, and remaining 1 cup water. Add this mixture to the saucepan. Bring the huckleberry mixture to a boil, stirring continuously, and cook until thickened. Stir the remaining 2 cups huckleberries into the filling, mixing until evenly distributed. Use the filling in your favorite pie or dessert recipes.

GRILLED MOOSE STEAKS
Serves 4 to 6

Moose meat is very lean. Some describe it as less stringy than beef, and it has a slightly sweet flavor to it. Wild game meat's taste can always vary depending on what the animal's diet has consisted of. This recipe requires some overnight setting, so prepare the night before.

2 pounds moose steaks
2 teaspoons meat tenderizer salt
1 (16-ounce) bottle Italian dressing
2 teaspoons paprika
Salt

Sprinkle both sides of the steaks with the meat tenderizer salt. Place the steaks and the dressing in a resealable plastic bag, seal tightly, and marinate in the refrigerator for at least 12 hours or up to 24 hours.

Preheat a grill to high. Remove the steaks and discard the marinade. Season the steaks on both sides with the paprika and salt, and grill for 3 to 4 minutes per side, depending on the thickness.

and the chance to live in a slightly less rural part of Montana than Rexford. It has since grown to two separate church districts comprised of almost forty-five families. There are a school and a meetinghouse where church services are held. Many of the Amish live in log homes.

The Mission General Store outside of town provides a place for the Amish, English (see page 11), and Native Americans to mingle. The store is perhaps the most prominent place for cultural exchanges. An Amish woman stands outside each Monday, selling homemade maple-frosted cinnamon rolls and dinner bread. "Those cinnamon rolls are to di-i-i-e for," one repeat customer said, eyeing the puffy, sweet treats.

In the early days of the St. Ignatius Amish community there wasn't much culinary comingling with the Native Americans. But there are some signs that the Amish and Native American culinary cultures may someday blend.

"I saw something in the paper the other day about a fry bread cook-off, and I thought to myself, I really would like to try to make fry bread," said resident Mary Troyer. This is a textbook example of how foods catch on within the Amish community. It's probably only a matter of time before fry bread is embraced and found showcased in Amish cookbooks and homemade Amish cinnamon rolls are enjoyed by the Native population.

EGGS LA GOLDEN
Serves 4

Many Amish and non-Amish in the St. Ignatius area enjoy raising their own free-range hens to provide a steady supply of fresh eggs. In St. Ignatius, though, grizzly bears occasionally wander down from the mountains and find hens to be a delicious snack. This causes the occasional confrontation between a grizzly bear and a homeowner. For homeowners Kathryn and John Miller, this egg recipe is a favorite for either breakfast or supper.

3 tablespoons shortening

2 tablespoons all-purpose flour

1 teaspoon salt

2 cups milk

6 hard-cooked eggs, whites separated
   and finely chopped, yolks reserved

Salt and black pepper

8 slices toast

Melt the shortening in a heavy saucepan over medium heat. Add the flour and salt, and stir until well blended. Slowly add the milk to the flour mixture, stirring constantly until a smooth sauce is formed.

Stir the chopped egg whites into the white sauce until evenly combined. Season the sauce with salt and pepper to taste. Arrange the toast slices on a platter and pour the white sauce over them. Mash the egg yolks through a sieve and sprinkle lightly over the sauce.

CAMPFIRE MEALS

The mountains and their abundance of wild game means plenty of outdoor meals. After an elk—an especially prized meat among Amish hunters—is caught, a delicious outdoor stew is often prepared. Ed and Brenda Beachy's family, which is originally from Ohio and runs a greenhouse and seed business, often prepares some delicious campfire "elk stews" over an open kettle in their yard. Many from their church will stop by for fellowship and a delicious meal. Mrs. Beachy admits that trying to make a formal recipe out of the meal is difficult, but she shared the ingredients: 5 pounds of tender elk roast, potatoes, carrots, onions, celery, whole-kernel corn, tiny precooked sausages called Smokies (sold in stores), cabbage, and green beans, all cooked over an open fire and seasoned with Cajun spices, thickened with flour, and simmered for hours. It makes for an enjoyable evening and fun meal for everyone.

MOUNTAIN PIE
Serves 1

Mountain pies, which are basically pizza-style sandwiches, are a favorite campfire food among the Montana Amish. The recipe requires sandwich irons (some call them hobo irons) to cook over the open flame, but you could make a home kitchen version of this in some commercially sold sandwich makers.

2 slices bread, buttered on one side
2 tablespoons pizza sauce
3 tablespoons shredded mozzarella cheese
Pizza toppings of your choice (mushrooms, beef, pepperoni, peppers, etc.)

Place 1 slice of the bread, buttered side down, onto an over-the-fire sandwich iron (or in a sandwich maker). Spread the pizza sauce evenly over the bread, then sprinkle the mozzarella over the sauce. Add any additional pizza toppings. Apply the second slice of bread, buttered side up, and clamp the sandwich iron closed. Put the sandwich iron into the campfire, and cook for about 2½ minutes on each side, or follow your sandwich maker's instructions. Carefully remove the sandwich from the iron and serve.

HUCKLEBERRY DELIGHT
Serves 8 to 10

Huckleberries have defied attempts at domestication. They are only found in the wild, high up in the mountains, and their scarcity can make them pricey, often selling for upward of forty dollars a gallon. In season, huckleberries are on the menu in many restaurants in Montana. Huckleberry milk shakes are a favorite, and this Huckleberry Delight is delicious.

1 (6-ounce) box blackberry or cherry gelatin mix

1 (20-ounce) can crushed pineapple

2 cups water

2 cups fresh huckleberries

8 ounces cream cheese

½ cup sugar

1 teaspoon vanilla extract

1 (8-ounce) container whipped topping, thawed

½ cup chopped walnuts (optional)

Combine the gelatin mix, pineapple, water, and huckleberries in a large mixing bowl. Stir until well combined, and spoon the mixture into a 9 by 13-inch glass baking dish.

In a separate bowl, combine the cream cheese, sugar, and vanilla. Beat with a mixer until well combined, then fold in the whipped topping. Spread this mixture evenly over the huckleberry mixture, and refrigerate until set. If desired, sprinkle with chopped walnuts before serving.

MONTANA OATMEAL COOKIES
Makes 2 to 3 dozen cookies

These are big cookies filled with flavor. Many Amish cooks use locally grown oats for these cookies and other recipes. Montana ranks among the nation's top producers of such grain crops as wheat, barley, and oats. Regular store-bought quick cooking oats can be used in this recipe. Since the frosting uses raw egg whites, you may want to omit the frosting if you have any concerns.

1 cup (2 sticks) butter, softened

3 cups firmly packed brown sugar

4 large eggs

2 teaspoons vanilla extract

1 teaspoon salt

2 teaspoons ground cinnamon

½ teaspoon ground nutmeg

3 cups all-purpose flour

3 cups quick-cooking oats

FROSTING

1¼ cups shortening

2 large egg whites, beaten

1 tablespoon vanilla extract

3 cups powdered sugar

Preheat the oven to 350°F.

Cream together the butter and brown sugar in a large mixing bowl. Add the eggs, one at a time, stirring well between each addition. Stir in the vanilla and mix until the mixture is creamy and light. Add the salt, cinnamon, nutmeg, flour, and oats to the wet ingredients. Stir until all of the dry ingredients are evenly incorporated and a dough is formed.

Drop the dough by tablespoons onto cookie sheets, then flatten with the bottom of a drinking glass dipped in water. Bake the cookies until golden brown around the edges, about 10 minutes. Allow the cookies to cool for about 5 minutes on the cookie sheets before transferring them to a wire rack to finish cooling.

Make the frosting: Combine the shortening, egg whites, and vanilla in a large mixing bowl and stir until the mixture is smooth and creamy. Gradually beat the powdered sugar into the shortening mix until a thick, smooth frosting is formed. Spread the frosting on top of the cooled cookies.

THE AMISH VS. THE INDIANS?

BY KEVIN WILLIAMS

When I first heard about the Amish settlement in St. Ignatius being located on the Flathead Indian Reservation, my imagination was captivated. I pictured two distinct peoples working and living together in culinary and cultural harmony. I was even hoping I'd find recipes for Amish fry bread and Indian whoopie pies. But after talking to a few Amish and a few Native Americans, my hopes were quickly dashed.

I have long, genuine affection for both cultures. I've been visiting Amish settlements since 1990. But I've also nurtured a longtime interest in our American indigenous people. Over the years, I've read such classics as Ian Frazier's *On the Rez* and Dee Brown's *Bury My Heart at Wounded Knee*. When I was a college freshman and budding journalist, I was captivated by a conflict involving the Quebec government and the Mohawk nation. I pitched a proposal to the editor of *Soldier of Fortune* magazine about going to northern New York to cover the increasingly violent feud between the Mohawk nation and state police. Some news media at the time described the situation as essentially a civil war.

So I was discouraged to learn that relations between the Amish and the Native Americans have not been the rosiest since the settlement was established.

On the surface, the two groups would seem to have more in common than not. Native Americans have a long, often justified, mistrust of outsiders. Their continent was stolen from them by European settlers. The Amish were chased out of Europe by religious fanatics who did not agree with their practice of adult baptism. There is a strain of Native American thought that they'd pretty much just like to be left alone to run their own affairs. The Amish also embrace that ideology. The Native Americans have certain legal protections based on sovereignty, protections that the Amish don't enjoy.

One didn't have to probe very deeply to uncover some animosity between the Amish and Native Americans.

"I just don't understand, why did they come here?" one Native American seethed. "I just don't like it when they come to our land, go into our mountains, and pick our huckleberries."

The historical irony was not lost on me. Here you have a group of people whose land was stolen from them, who were forced onto reservations, who were double-crossed and swindled by a parade of presidents, and who now feel that the Amish are trampling on their land. Could a really small group—maybe four hundred people at most—on a reservation the size of Rhode Island really be having an impact?

According to tribal officials, yes.

The Flathead Indian Reservation comprises 1.3 million acres, of which approximately 700,000 are owned by the tribe.

"All fishing and hunting activities are under the control of the tribe," said Tom McDonald. "Tribal culture teaches us: Don't take it unless you can eat it or use it."

Another problem, according to the tribe, is that out of all the places the Amish chose to live on the reservation, they picked one of the most ecologically sensitive areas. "The Amish moved into the buffer zone," McDonald said, describing the foothills as a haven for wolves, eagles, bears, and other endangered species.

The tribe and the Amish have been reaching out to one another in an effort to understand one another better. I hope to see the two groups celebrate their commonalities and share the land as stewards in the years ahead.

SAN LUIS VALLEY, COLORADO

AT A GLANCE

Date established: 2002

Number of church districts: 2

Culinary highlights: Hispanic food

Stretching from south-central Colorado into northern New Mexico, the San Luis Valley, at over 120 miles in length, is the largest intermountain valley in the world. The scrubby desert valley is ringed by the Sangre de Cristo Mountains to the east and the San Juan Mountains to the west. *Sangre de Cristo* means "blood of Christ" in Spanish, and the area's Hispanic roots run deep and that reflects on Amish menus.

Resident Rose Ellen Yoder describes the high-altitude valley as "very good for our horse-farming ways" with plenty of warm days and cool nights. The Amish here enjoy a slower pace of life than in the bustling tourist enclaves of Ohio, Indiana, and Pennsylvania. The settlement started in May 2002, with the first church services held on July 21 of that year. The community grew quickly and is now divided into north and south districts, with two schools, the aptly named Mountain View and Antelope Run. As the school name suggests, the valley is plentiful with elk, mule deer, and white-tailed deer.

The Amish in the area enjoy a diversified economy. Businesses include a few carpenter crews, farmers, buggy repair shops, a harness shop, a cabinet shop, a window shop, a woodworking shop, truss shops, greenhouses, a bakery, and a jam and jelly shop. There is also a salvage store in the community. Buggies are black, but they are in all different styles, because the Amish in the San Luis Valley come from a variety of settlements.

The beauty of the valley seems to evoke the most satisfaction. "It is unusual to not see the sun shine every day. Many awesome sunrises and sunsets are seen here," Yoder said.

Spring in the valley is often windy, with summers punctuated by monsoon rains that arrive in July. The area has a dry climate, averaging only 7 to 10 inches of rain a year, most of it during the summer monsoon season. Autumn brings rainbows that arc across the valley. And while the warmth of the valley insulates most inhabitants from snowy winters, the surrounding mountains do get capped heavily with white. The spring snowmelt then feeds the canals, which the Amish use to irrigate.

Life is very busy during the August canning season. Rose Ellen Yoder describes the days as quite full as "garden goodies get ready in the latter part of July, all of August, and into September." Plus most of the Amish residents of this settlement receive their annual supply of peaches, pears, and other fruits to can or freeze.

By 2012, Colorado was becoming an increasingly popular destination for Amish adventurers from out east. As the Amish population grows, so, too, will the culinary culture, but the early years have given menus a decidedly south-of-the-border flair.

PANCAKES
Serves 8 to 10

No Amish cook is without a simple pancake recipe. This one is a favorite among the Amish in Colorado.

3 large eggs, beaten

3 cups milk

¼ cup vegetable oil

3 cups all-purpose flour

1½ teaspoons salt

7 teaspoons baking powder

Combine the eggs, milk, and oil in a large mixing bowl. Add the flour, salt, and baking powder. Mix until all the ingredients are thoroughly combined, to form a batter. Drop the batter by quarter-cupfuls onto a hot, greased griddle. Cook until the edges are set and bubbles break the surface, about 1 minute. Flip the pancakes and continue cooking until golden brown and cooked through.

THE AMISH COOK'S WESTERN OBSERVATIONS

BY LOVINA EICHER

Reading about all the wild game in the western settlements was interesting. We do use wild game in our cooking, but, of course, the game out here is different, although some do hunt bear in northern Michigan. Around here we use our deer meat in summer sausage, homemade deer jerky, and tenderloins. I make casseroles and soups with ground deer meat, and it also makes really good homemade sloppy joes. We sometimes mix venison with sausage or bacon to make it a little greasier.

I'm sure my husband, Joe, would like the fishing out there, too! Fresh fish is a favorite in this household, but we have different types here: Bluegill, bass, and perch are found in area lakes. I like to roll it in a homemade batter of flour, egg, and butter, then deep-fry it.

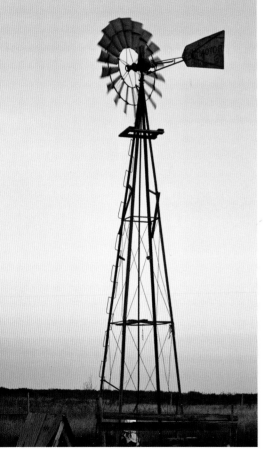

WET BURRITOS
Serves 4 to 6

Wet burritos are eaten with a fork, not with your hand. As the name implies, the dish is a cheesy, melty mess, not conducive for fingers but great for forks.

1 pound ground beef

1 tablespoon taco seasoning

1 (16-ounce) can pinto beans

2 tablespoons chopped onion

1 (10.75-ounce) can cream of mushroom soup

⅓ cup salad dressing, such as Miracle Whip, or ½ cup sour cream

6 Flour Tortillas (page 167)

1 cup shredded Cheddar cheese

Salsa, for serving (see Note)

Preheat the oven to 325°F.

Brown the ground meat in a medium skillet over medium heat. Drain off the grease, then add the taco seasoning, beans, and onion. In a medium bowl, mix the mushroom soup and salad dressing until the mixture is smooth. Pour the soup mixture over the meat mixture, and combine thoroughly.

Place two tortillas on the bottom of a 2-quart casserole dish, followed by a layer of one-third of the meat mixture. Continue layering until all the ingredients have been used, ending with the meat mixture on top. Sprinkle the shredded cheese on top of everything. Bake until the casserole is bubbling and the cheese is melted, about 30 minutes. Serve with salsa, if desired.

Note: You can use your favorite store-bought salsa, or the recipe on page 70.

FLOUR TORTILLAS
Makes 12 to 15 tortillas

Colorado has a growing Hispanic population, and its foods are definitely making their way into Amish homes in the area. Here's one.

4 cups all-purpose flour

2 teaspoons baking powder

1 teaspoon salt

½ cup lard

1 cup water

Place the flour, baking powder, and salt in a large mixing bowl and stir until the ingredients are thoroughly combined. Using a pastry blender or your hands, cut the lard into the dry ingredients until the mixture is crumbly. Stir in the water, kneading as necessary, to form a dough. Allow the dough to rest for 30 minutes.

Form the dough into twelve to fifteen balls. On a lightly floured surface, roll out each ball to about ⅛-inch thickness. Cook each tortilla on a hot, ungreased griddle until browned and no longer doughy in appearance, 1 to 2 minutes per side.

# METRIC CONVERSIONS AND EQUIVALENTS

METRIC CONVERSION FORMULAS

TO CONVERT	MULTIPLY
Ounces to grams	Ounces by 28.35
Pounds to kilograms	Pounds by 0.454
Teaspoons to milliliters	Teaspoons by 4.93
Tablespoons to milliliters	Tablespoons by 14.79
Fluid ounces to milliliters	Fluid ounces by 29.57
Cups to milliliters	Cups by 236.59
Cups to liters	Cups by 0.236
Pints to liters	Pints by 0.473
Quarts to liters	Quarts by 0.946
Gallons to liters	Gallons by 3.785
Inches to centimeters	Inches by 2.54

APPROXIMATE METRIC EQUIVALENTS

VOLUME

¼ teaspoon	1 milliliter
½ teaspoon	2.5 milliliters
¾ teaspoon	4 milliliters
1 teaspoon	5 milliliters
1¼ teaspoons	6 milliliters
1½ teaspoons	7.5 milliliters
1¾ teaspoons	8.5 milliliters
2 teaspoons	10 milliliters
1 tablespoon (½ fluid ounce)	15 milliliters
2 tablespoons (1 fluid ounce)	30 milliliters
¼ cup	60 milliliters
⅓ cup	80 milliliters
½ cup (4 fluid ounces)	120 milliliters
⅔ cup	160 milliliters
¾ cup	180 milliliters
1 cup (8 fluid ounces)	240 milliliters
1¼ cups	300 milliliters
1½ cups (12 fluid ounces)	360 milliliters
1⅔ cups	400 milliliters
2 cups (1 pint)	460 milliliters
3 cups	700 milliliters
4 cups (1 quart)	0.95 liter
1 quart plus ¼ cup	1 liter
4 quarts (1 gallon)	3.8 liters

WEIGHT

¼ ounce	7 grams
½ ounce	14 grams
¾ ounce	21 grams
1 ounce	28 grams
1¼ ounces	35 grams
1½ ounces	42.5 grams
1⅔ ounces	45 grams
2 ounces	57 grams
3 ounces	85 grams
4 ounces (¼ pound)	113 grams
5 ounces	142 grams
6 ounces	170 grams
7 ounces	198 grams
8 ounces (½ pound)	227 grams
16 ounces (1 pound)	454 grams
35.25 ounces (2.2 pounds)	1 kilogram

LENGTH

⅛ inch	3 millimeters
¼ inch	6 millimeters
½ inch	1.25 centimeters
1 inch	2.5 centimeters
2 inches	5 centimeters
2½ inches	6 centimeters
4 inches	10 centimeters
5 inches	13 centimeters
6 inches	15.25 centimeters
12 inches (1 foot)	30 centimeters

COMMON INGREDIENTS AND THEIR APPROXIMATE EQUIVALENTS

1 cup uncooked rice = 225 grams

1 cup all-purpose flour = 140 grams

1 stick butter (4 ounces • ½ cup • 8 tablespoons) = 110 grams

1 cup butter (8 ounces • 2 sticks • 16 tablespoons) = 220 grams

1 cup brown sugar, firmly packed = 225 grams

1 cup granulated sugar = 200 grams

OVEN TEMPERATURES

To convert Fahrenheit to Celsius, subtract 32 from Fahrenheit, multiply the result by 5, then divide by 9.

DESCRIPTION	FAHRENHEIT	CELSIUS	BRITISH GAS MARK
Very cool	200°	95°	0
Very cool	225°	110°	¼
Very cool	250°	120°	½
Cool	275°	135°	1
Cool	300°	150°	2
Warm	325°	165°	3
Moderate	350°	175°	4
Moderately hot	375°	190°	5
Fairly hot	400°	200°	6
Hot	425°	220°	7
Very hot	450°	230°	8
Very hot	475°	245°	9

Information compiled from a variety of sources, including *Recipes into Type* by Joan Whitman and Dolores Simon (Newton, MA: Biscuit Books, 2000); *The New Food Lover's Companion* by Sharon Tyler Herbst (Hauppauge, NY: Barron's, 1995); and *Rosemary Brown's Big Kitchen Instruction Book* (Kansas City, MO: Andrews McMeel, 1998).

INDEX